Where Are You?

Where Are You?

Finding Yourself in the Bible

Josh Franklin

WIPF & STOCK · Eugene, Oregon

WHERE ARE YOU?
Finding Yourself in the Bible

Wipf & Stock
An Imprint of Wipf and Stock Publishers
199 W. 8th Ave., Suite 3
Eugene, OR 97401

www.wipfandstock.com

PAPERBACK ISBN: 979-8-3852-6838-2
HARDCOVER ISBN: 979-8-3852-6839-9
EBOOK ISBN: 979-8-3852-6840-5

VERSION NUMBER 02/06/26

Scriptural quotations from the Hebrew Bible are the author's translation unless otherwise noted.

Contents

Acknowledgments

EVERY BOOK BEGINS WITH a spark of inspiration, but it takes a community to keep that spark alive. This one grew out of conversations, classrooms, questions, and countless cups of coffee shared with people who helped me see Torah—and myself—more deeply.

Foremost among them is Rabbi Alan Ullman, a master teacher and, perhaps, the best teacher of Torah most people have never heard of. Early in my rabbinate, I wandered into one of his Torah classes not knowing what to expect and walked out changed. The way he approached sacred text—as a mirror for our own souls and a guide for how we live—reshaped the way I think, teach, and write. Many of the ideas in this book trace their roots back to his classes and his friendship. His feedback and insight throughout the writing process were nothing short of transformative.

I am grateful to my colleagues and friends Rabbi Marc Katz, Rabbi Sonja Pilz, Rabbi Leon Morris, and Rabbi Larry Hoffman, each of whom offered generous feedback and conversation that helped me find clarity in moments of creative uncertainty.

A special note of gratitude to Steven Gaines, who believed there was a book in me before I did. His encouragement, his keen editorial eye, and his belief in the importance of this project guided me from the first rough pages to the finished manuscript.

To the Jewish Center of the Hamptons community: thank you for granting me the gift of time and space during my sabbatical to begin writing. That period of reflection was a blessing I could only embark on because of your trust and generosity. Thank you as well for being a congregation so open to my Torah teaching, for engaging with depth and curiosity, and for creating a spiritual home where I have been able to learn, reflect, and grow alongside you.

I am deeply appreciative of Wipf and Stock Publishers, whose belief in this project brought it from vision to reality and who entrusted me with the privilege of seeing it published as my first book.

And finally, to my wife, Stephanie, and our daughters, Lilah and Amelia—you are the heart of everything I do. Thank you for your love, patience, and the grace you offered each time I disappeared behind a screen or a stack of notes. My hope is that one day, when Lilah and Amelia are older, they will open these pages to explore the depths of Torah wisdom and that within them they might find not only words of guidance but echoes of my love—a light to accompany them through the unfolding journey of their lives.

Introduction

FROM THE VAST COLLECTION of Hasidic tales and parables, I find myself particularly drawn to a legend that has captivated me for many years. It revolves around a rabbi unjustly imprisoned and awaiting trial. As the rabbi languishes behind bars, the chief of police visits him, seizing the chance to mock him with questions about the Bible. The chief of police shows a particular intrigue for the story of Adam in the garden of Eden. After Adam and Eve eat the forbidden fruit from the tree of knowledge within Eden, Adam realizes his nakedness and attempts to hide. God calls out to Adam, "Where are you?" (Gen 3:9). The chief of police finds himself puzzled by the concept of an omniscient God inquiring about Adam's whereabouts, suggesting a potential flaw in God's all-knowing nature.[1] The rabbi's response not only leaves the chief in awe but also reflects on how we might interpret this part of the Bible in our lives: "The question isn't about your physical location in the world but rather 'where are you in *your* world?'" This story goes beyond a simple game of hide and seek, highlighting that God's question to Adam isn't for God's enlightenment but for Adam's benefit. The profound inquiry "where are you?" acts as a universal call to self-reflection, urging us, much like Adam, to face the realities we often avoid. It prompts us to look beyond our facades, stirring deep reflection about our identity and our place in the journey of life.

1. Buber, *Way of Man*, loc 140–47.

Adam's actual response to God feels quite pathetic: "I heard your voice in the garden, and I was afraid because I am naked. So I hid" (Gen 3:10). Most of the biblical patriarchs like Abraham, Jacob, and Moses offer the holy response "*hineini*" to God's call, which means "I am here, I am present, and I am ready." Perhaps Adam, like the chief of police, doesn't really understand the nature of the question. In his fear, he thinks God is actually asking about where he is hiding. What he fails to realize is that God's question is meant for Adam's self-reflection. God cares little about where Adam hides; God wants to know why Adam hides. Like Adam, we far too often evade answering the question "where are you?" because we fear the honest answer. We want to say that we are present, but really we are distracted by our phones, the crushing stresses of work, failing marriages, unrealized career goals, and vices that lead us astray from where we ought to be. Adam's fear of God stems from his shame of disobeying God and falling short of God's expectations. It's much easier to hide than to say, "I am in a place of shame."

It sounds so simple to respond to God's call by saying "*hineini*, I am here." What's so hard about uttering one word? Nothing! *Hineini*, however, is more than a word, and it's not just something you can say, it's an expression of utter vulnerability. It's about going all in on a relationship. What Adam fails to learn is that it's only when we have the courage to show our shame, our brokenness, our imperfections, and our authentic selves that we forge sacred connections with those around us, and with God. Instead of expressing *hineini*, Adam deflects the blame for his sin upon Eve and upon God and says, "The woman that *you* placed with me, it was she that gave to me [the fruit] from the tree, and so I ate it" (Gen 3:12). Adam not only hid from God when God called, "Where are you?"—Adam hides from himself even as God confronts him about his indiscretion. Adam conveys the antithesis of *hineini*, exhibiting a guarded demeanor, seeking refuge in concealment from God, thereby illustrating a withdrawal from the openness and receptivity that define true presence and connection. *Hineini* is more than just showing up physically; it requires active listening and responding to the call of the other, whether the call comes from God or from our friends, family, and those we care about.

When later in the Bible, Moses—the great leader of the Israelites—stands at the foot of Mount Sinai, ready to receive the Torah, God calls out to him and says "go up the mountain and be there" (Exod 24:12). Many notice that the words "be there" are superfluous. We might imagine that Moses should only have to ascend the mountain to receive Torah, but the extra words convey another layer of presence. Rabbi Menachem Mendel of Kotzk (1787–1859) taught, "If Moses went up to the mountain, of course he would be there. However, this is proof that a person can exert tremendous effort to reach the top of a mountain . . . but his head may be elsewhere. The main thing is not the ascent, but being there, and only there."[2] That is, Moses can only receive Torah when he can express *hineini*, being present not just physically but emotionally and spiritually as well. It is up to each of us to hear the sacred question in our lives: "Where are you?" And our responsibility lies in coming forth fully with *hineini*, being able to answer the question with "yes, here I am, bare and unshielded, open to both the pain and the joy of true connection."

AYEKAH: BEYOND GEOGRAPHIC SPACE

Where are you? As I write, I sit at my desk, surrounded by books and notes. But my geographic location doesn't even begin to answer the question. As the rabbi in the Hasidic legend subtly points out, it's not about "where are you in the world?" but rather "where are you in *your* world?" The former poses an inquiry about geography and the latter about your emotional and spiritual state of mind. God cares little about tracking us and pinpointing our physical location. But God does care about what our hearts feel. As the Psalmist writes, God "looks within us, and knows us" (Ps 139:1). Jeremiah echoes this understanding of God's search within us: "I YHWH probe the heart and search the mind" (Jer 17:10).

2. Greenberg, *Torah Gems*, 165.

When God asks us "where are you?," God offers us a platform to express *hineini*.

While most of the time we might know our own physical location, we too often sit bewildered in the dark when it comes to knowing and understanding the emotions we are experiencing. We like to think that we own our emotions, and that we fully comprehend the complexities of our subconscious. More likely, it takes another to help us understand what should be obvious but never is. The screenwriter Aaron Sorkin underscores this idea in several of his shows by placing the smartest person in the room into a psychiatrist's office and giving the viewers a sense of how the world's most intelligent people can also be oblivious to their own obvious emotional baggage. In the episode of *The West Wing* entitled "Night Five," President Jed Bartlet suffers from insomnia due to a conversation about his abusive father with his staffer Toby Ziegler. We as the viewer understand that President Bartlet's psychosis stems from his trying to please his deceased father who hated him because his son was smarter than him. The psychiatrist begins his analysis by going through a litany of pro forma questions about possible environmental, physical, and lifestyle factors, yet we as the viewers already know the obvious truth that only the president has trouble seeing. As much as the psychiatrist tries to show President Bartlet that the his problem is rooted in his father's abuse, Bartlet struggles to come to grips with what everyone else around him knows. The conversation concludes by the president, remarking, "I'm not trying to get my father to like me"; the psychiatrist immediately strikes back at the nerve the president is so desperately trying to guard: "Good, because it's never, never going to happen!"[3] The process of exploring the president's agita is really a painful and a prolonged exploration of the question "*ayekah?*" Expressing *hineini* might not feel comfortable or instinctive, but it's often exactly what we need to grow.

Take as another example of the complexity of emotions, a scene from the pop-culture fiction series *Harry Potter*. In the book *Harry Potter and the Order of the Phoenix*, Harry Potter has

3. *West Wing*, "Night Five."

a romantic encounter with a classmate named Cho Chang. As they kiss, Cho begins to cry, and Harry can't quite wrap his adolescent head around Cho's reaction. Harry jumps to the conclusion that perhaps he's a bad kisser, but his friend Hermione Granger offers him a deeper insight into the web of tangled emotions that may have caused Cho to shed tears:

> Well, obviously, she's feeling very sad, because of Cedric dying. Then I expect she's feeling confused because she liked Cedric and now she likes Harry, and she can't work out who she likes best. Then she'll be feeling guilty, thinking it's an insult to Cedric's memory to be kissing Harry at all, and she'll be worrying about what everyone else might say about her if she starts going out with Harry. And she probably can't work out what her feelings toward Harry are anyway, because he was the one who was with Cedric when Cedric died, so that's all very mixed up and painful. Oh, and she's afraid she's going to be thrown off the Ravenclaw Quidditch team because she's been flying so badly.[4]

You don't have to know all the referenced characters or magical terms in Hermione's analysis to understand that Cho carries a great deal of emotional trauma that she likely hasn't fully processed. Most teenagers aren't capable of confronting their own feelings; what's more, Harry lacks the emotional intelligence to recite the magical Hebrew word to Cho that would help him overcome his adolescent awkwardness. *Ayekah*—where are you?

I've already introduced a bold concept: the question "*ayekah*" carries implications beyond space; it also probes the state of one's mind. Additionally, I want to incorporate another dimension into this idea. When you think you're dealing with geography in the Bible, you may actually be dealing with something else entirely. While the names of places described in the Bible often represent very real locations, they sometimes also signify something deeper, a metaphysical emotional space—a realm beyond the physical, dealing with the nature of existence, identity, and the soul—that

4. Rowling, *Order of the Phoenix*, 459–60.

each person throughout their life cycles through. This is distinct from the metaphorical, which draws comparisons to convey meaning; the metaphysical engages with the very real and palpable truths of human experience. Sometimes, the name of a place bears zero correlation to any physical location. The modern mind may be concerned about landscape, but the Bible better charts lifescape the different stages and emotional periods that each cycle through in our time on this earth.

Geography is not irrelevant in the Bible; rather, there is an additional layer to how we should approach its reading. Too often, people become fixated on a literal interpretation of the text, as though its words are meant to chronicle history in a modern sense. However, it's worth noting that the word for "history" doesn't even exist in biblical Hebrew. This means that the biblical authors could not have conceived of the world through a historical paradigm for which their language lacked the vocabulary.

The concept of history as we understand it originated with the Greeks. It was a field of study developed to analyze the past through the recording and examination of data. Herodotus, who lived in the 5th century BCE, is often referred to as the "Father of History" because he applied a systematic method to the study of historical events. His work *The Histories* chronicled prominent kings and famous battles such as Marathon, Thermopylae, Artemisium, Salamis, Plataea, and Mycale.

The Bible, however, belongs to a different genre. While it narrates events of the past, its primary concern is not with historical accuracy but with memory and meaning. In fact, the closest biblical Hebrew word to "history" is *zechirah* (זכירה), which translates to something like "remembrance." The Bible is less a record of what happened and more a reflection of how we derive meaning from our collective memory of the past. It offers a spiritual and moral framework for understanding our origins and our relationship with the Divine, rather than a factual account of historical events. In a similar vein, the Bible uses geography to ground its stories in tangible settings, but its focus is not on mapping the land with accuracy. Instead, geography often serves as a canvas for portraying life experience.

A NOTE ON TRANSLATION AND THE DIVINE NAME

Unless otherwise noted, all translations of the Hebrew Bible and rabbinic texts—including Midrash, Talmud, Zohar, and classical commentaries—are my own. My aim is not to replace existing translations but to listen closely to the language of our sacred texts and bring forward the subtle layers of meaning that are often lost in English. Because much of this book explores the etymology of Hebrew words, I often preserve the transliteration of key Hebrew terms within the translation itself. At times these words will stand untranslated; at others, a parenthetical explanation will follow. I do this not to burden the reader but to allow the Hebrew to breathe—to let its sound and texture linger on the page as part of the teaching.

In translating, I have also sought to use gender-neutral language for God. This reflects my conviction that the Divine transcends human categories. While the Hebrew language operates within a gendered grammatical structure, I do not believe that God possesses gender. Any pronoun risks confinement; the Holy One defies any and all boundaries. My hope is that, by freeing the text from gendered language, readers might encounter the Divine not as a projection of the human but as the boundless source of all life.

Throughout this book, I render the four-letter name of God, the Tetragrammaton, as YHWH. In Jewish tradition, this name is never pronounced as written. It emerges from the Hebrew root *h-y-h*, "to be," suggesting the mystery of existence itself—Being that was, is, and will be. By preserving these four consonants, I seek to honor both the reverence and the ineffability of that name. It reminds us that the Divine cannot be fully spoken, only approached with humility and awe.

These choices—of translation, transliteration, and theology—are themselves an expression of the book's central question:

Where are you? For to translate is to locate oneself in relation to the sacred text, to stand between the seen and the unseen, and to listen for the Voice that still calls our name.

THE JOURNEY AHEAD

Throughout the chapters that follow, we will journey through an array of biblical landscapes, each offering profound insights into our spiritual and emotional lives. In chapter one, we step into the garden of Eden, the mythic paradise that has sparked millennia of attempts to locate it on a map, though its significance reaches far beyond any physical place. Chapter two takes us to Mount Sinai, where Moses received the Torah and the Israelites stood at the heart of divine revelation. In chapter three, we arrive at Haran, a place with a marked presence on the map yet imbued with meaning that transcends its geographic coordinates. Chapter four guides us into the *Midbar*, the wilderness—a liminal space where we grapple with emotional and physical uncertainty. In chapter five, we descend into *Mitzrayim*, the land of Egypt. Here, we explore its dual reality as both a physical location and a metaphysical state of constraint, revealing that Egypt is often closer than we think. Chapter six brings us to Mara, the bitter waters of the wilderness, where the Israelites wrestled with hardship and doubt. Chapter seven takes us into *Golah*, the exile, where we experience the pain and growth of being displaced from our homeland. Finally, in chapter eight, we gather at the well, a recurring biblical meeting place where encounters with each other and with God unfold in transformative ways.

These chapters offer a glimpse into the rich landscape of biblical geography, both physical and metaphysical. They provide a lens through which we can see the deeper truths of the text and perhaps uncover a terrain you never realized was there. While the landscapes explored here are but a few, their resonance extends far beyond, offering a way to see biblical texts that reverberate across the biblical narrative and into our lives.

1

Where Is Eden?

> There was once a king's son who had a larger and more beautiful collection of books than any one else in the world, and full of splendid copper-plate engravings. He could read and obtain information respecting every people of every land; but not a word could he find to explain the situation of the garden of paradise, and this was just what he most wished to know.
>
> —Hans Christian Andersen, "The Garden of Paradise"[1]

This excerpt from a fairy tale echoes a very real fascination that explorers, theologians, and academics have had for centuries about the geographic location of the garden of Eden. The scant clues found in the opening chapters of the biblical book of Genesis invite a world of wild interpretations and hypotheses, each more fantastical and speculative than the next.

Christopher Columbus, while exploring the New World in 1498, became convinced that he had stumbled upon the entrance to the garden of Eden at the mouth of the 1,700-mile Orinoco River, in

1. Andersen, *Garden of Paradise*, loc 40–44.

what is now modern-day Venezuela. Writing to King Ferdinand and Queen Isabella, he described the river's grandeur: "If the water does not proceed from the earthly paradise, it seems to be a still greater wonder, for I do not believe that there is any river in the world so large and deep." Columbus believed that following the river inland would lead to a mountain shaped like a giant breast, with the garden of Eden located at its center—the nipple. Yet, despite his bold claims, Columbus never ventured up the river to see this biblical paradise for himself. He rationalized his hesitation by stating, "No one can go [to earthly Paradise] but by God's permission."[2]

Unlike Columbus, William Fairfield Warren wasn't an explorer but a scholar—the first president of Boston University and a trained Methodist minister. In 1885, Warren proposed an even more wild theory in his book *Paradise Found.* He argued that the cradle of civilization was not in the tropics or even sub-Saharan Africa but at the North Pole. According to Warren, the garden of Eden lay hidden in this uncharted Arctic expanse, waiting to be discovered.

Tse Tsan Tai, an early 20th-century theorist, pushed the search for Eden to new extremes, proposing that the fabled paradise was located in China—specifically, in a crescent-shaped oasis in the Mongolian desert known as Chinese Turkestan. From there, the quest for Eden spiraled outward, with theories multiplying and spreading across the globe. Proposed locations include Iraq, Turkey, Sri Lanka, the Seychelles, Florida, California, Missouri, Ohio, Egypt, Sweden, and beyond—each claim more imaginative than the last.

These theories were rooted in the belief that the names of places mentioned in the Bible always correspond to actual coordinates on the globe. But even early commentators on the Bible recognized that Eden wasn't meant to be an actual physical location. The Hellenistic Jewish philosopher Philo viewed Eden as a metaphor for the human soul. He interpreted the story allegorically, suggesting that the garden represents the intellect or divine wisdom. The Zohar, a book of Jewish mysticism, associates the garden of Eden and the river that issues forth from it as cosmic emanations of the various parts of God (Zohar 1:135b). Similarly,

2. Quoted in Wilensky-Lanford, *Paradise Lust*, 16.

the Christian theologian Origen (c. 185–253 CE), in his work *De Principiis*, viewed the garden of Eden allegorically, suggesting that the rivers and the garden symbolize spiritual truths and the state of the human soul in its ideal relationship with God. Origen went so far as to label those who view the text literally from Genesis as fools. He writes:

> Who is found so ignorant as to suppose that God, as if He had been a husbandman, planted trees in paradise, in Eden towards the east, and a tree of life in it, i.e., a visible and palpable tree of wood, so that anyone eating of it with bodily teeth should obtain life, and, eating again of another tree, should come to the knowledge of good and evil? No one, I think, can doubt that the statement that God walked in the afternoon in paradise, and that Adam lay hid under a tree, is related figuratively in Scripture, that some mystical meaning may be indicated by it.[3]

If Eden cannot be found on a map, we are left with a profound question: Where, then, does it truly exist?

EDEN OFF THE MAP

Perusing the sacred narratives of the Bible, it becomes evident that the names of places woven into its pages defy the confines of conventional maps. "YHWH God planted a garden in Eden, which is in the east, and placed there the man that God created" (Gen 2:8). Like the many explorers and theologians who view the Bible literally, we might be inclined to try and uncover the geographic location of this place. In doing so, you will inevitably hit an insurmountable hurdle. The Bible tells us that a river issues from Eden and breaks off into four different rivers. The first river is called the Pishon and is generally understood to be the Nile River.[4] The second river is

3. Origen, *On First Principles*, §314.

4. The commentator Rashi (1040–1105 CE) notes that "פישון Pishon is the Nile, the River of Egypt. Because its waters grow plentiful and rise and water the land, it is called Pishon, the name being of the same root as the verb in (Hab 1:8) ופשו פרשיו "and their horsemen increased."

Gihon, and it surrounds the land of Cush.[5] The third and fourth rivers are most easily identifiable: they are the Hiddekel, which is the Tigris, and the Perat, which is the Euphrates. Theoretically, to find the location of Eden, one would only need to find the point of intersection of these four rivers. The problem is that although the Tigris and Euphrates do indeed intersect, they do not converge with the Nile, and both reside far from the Nile or any potential locations of the Gihon River. We should not misconstrue this as evidence against the reality of Eden; rather, it exists in a different kind of spiritual plane that cannot be found on Google Maps. Perhaps we should understand Eden in the same light that Sir Thomas More understood the idea when he coined the word "Utopia" for his 1516 book title. Utopia describes an idyllic and imaginary island but most importantly, he gives us the etymology of *ou topos*, meaning "no place" or "nowhere."[6]

In his collection of essays, *Map Is Not Territory*, Jonathan Z. Smith distinguishes "between a locative vision of the world (which emphasizes place) and a Utopian vision of the world (using the term in its strict sense: the value of being in no place)."[7] According to Smith, the biblical literature primarily leans towards locative visions. While I value his distinction between different visions of how we understand biblical geography, I believe that Smith got it backwards. The Bible intends us to have a utopian vision of the world, that is, a view in which place transcends physical geography and inclines us to see places as life experience as opposed to marks on a map. In this utopian vision, Eden is not bound by earthly limitations, and its significance lies not in its geographical location but in the profound spiritual and existential truths it embodies. Just as Sir Thomas More's "Utopia" describes an idyllic imaginary island, so too does Eden beckon us to a place that is "nowhere" on

5. Commentators have struggled to identify a river that meets the description described in the text. Some place it as an Asiatic River that may be the Oxus, the Orontes, or the Ganges. Medieval commentators who follow the Septuagint, the Greek translation of the Bible, considered Cush to be Ethiopia, making the Gihon an African river.

6. More, *Utopia*.

7. Smith, *Map Is Not Territory*, 10.

a map but is very much real in the depths of our understanding and interpretation.

So where do we look for Eden? Like many biblical names, the key to unlocking where we might find Eden comes from its namesake. Eden in Hebrew, ע-ד-ן, means delight or pleasure. The garden of Eden is really the place of the garden of delight. When the biblical matriarch Sarah, the wife of Abraham, first hears that she will get pregnant in her old age, Sarah laughs and says, "After I have become worn, can I still have pleasure (*ednah*)?" Notice the word she uses for pleasure, *ednah,* a clear echo of Eden. Put another way, she's really asking, "Can I really experience Eden at this stage of my life?" The answer is unequivocally yes! Many of us believe that life's peak experiences are reserved for our later years. However, as we age, we often lament that the best parts of life occurred in the past, thus missing out at both stages. The gateway to Eden can manifest anywhere in the world, and crucially, at any moment in our lives. Adam and Eve were not the only people to experience Eden; they were just the first to do so. We have the potential to experience the garden of delight wherever and whenever we might be; we simply need to stop looking at maps and start looking at ourselves.

Within Jewish tradition, a captivating text envisions Eden as a realm of the afterlife, a destination awaiting us upon our mortal departure. As the esteemed rabbinic sage Yochanan Ben Zakkai lies on his deathbed, he contemplates, "Before me are two paths: one leads to the garden of Eden, and one leads to Gehenna,[8] and I do not know on which I'm being led" (Berachot 28b). According to the sages, the righteous souls shall be welcomed into the blissful embrace of Eden, while the wicked souls shall endure Gehenna's torments, a realm of penance preceding final judgment. While the conception of Eden as afterlife feels consistent with a place without a distinct location, I believe we find Eden not after life but within life.

8. The name "Gehenna" stems from Gey-Hinom, the Valley of Hinom, located to the west of ancient Jerusalem. There, it was common practice for people would sacrifice children, and it thus became associated with the worst place imaginable. The rabbis associated it with the place where the wicked go after they die to suffer.

The enchanting lyrics of the song "Somewhere Over the Rainbow," written for the legendary 1939 film *The Wizard of Oz*, capture the essence of the quest for an Eden beyond the realm of the physical world. Before singing, Dorothy speaks of a blissful place where there are no troubles—a place one cannot reach by ordinary means, somewhere far beyond the familiar sky. The song paints a vision of a world where worries melt away, where happiness and harmony prevail—a picturesque utopia where skies are always blue and dreams come true. It has become an iconic and beloved anthem that continues to resonate with listeners, inspiring them to envision a brighter tomorrow and hold onto the power of imagination and optimism. Despite the wonders and adventures she experiences in the land of Oz, Dorothy's ultimate goal is to return to Kansas, for she comes to realize that her Eden lies in the familiarity and comfort of home. To reach that place, all she must do is click her heels and affirm, "There's no place like home." The home she seeks is not merely a physical location but a state of mind and heart. It represents the emotional connection and attachment we have to the native elements of our lives.

We find the garden of Eden in the midst of life's most sacred moments. When we glimpse Eden, time seems suspended, and our bodies sense a synesthetic symphony of overwhelming delight. Eden is the embrace of a sunset's golden hues, the gentle caress of a loved one's touch, and the whisper of a kindred soul's wisdom. Eden comes in the cascade of laughter that ripples through our very being and the warmth that permeates our hearts when a stranger shows us an abundance of compassion. In these transcendent encounters, the veil between heaven and earth grows thin and the mundane fades away. In this sanctuary of delight, we dance in harmony with the universe, fully aware of our connection to God's embracing presence. When we truly perceive God's love for us in a moment of profound realization, we are in the heart of Eden. Similarly, when we engage deeply and vulnerably with another, creating a space of mutual presence and shared vulnerability, it is as if we have stepped into Eden. These might only be momentary glimpses of paradise, yet these fleeting instances craft memories that stay with us. The garden of Eden is not a distant memory or a mythic afterlife but a boundless wellspring of delight that we discover throughout our lives.

Shabbat, according to the rabbinic sages, gives us a taste of the garden of Eden (Berachot 57b). In this intersection of sacred space and time, the stresses of the outside world fade away. Each and every week, my family gathers around the Shabbat dinner table with our friends and extended family. A serene ambiance engulfs the air, setting the stage for an experience that often brings me to Eden. I relish the soft glow of shabbat candles, the rhythmic cadence of prayers and blessings, and the aroma of my wife's freshly baked challah. We strive to craft a gateway to Eden, though achieving this spiritual union demands more than mere preparation. There are evenings when chaos intrudes—a child's tantrum shatters the mood, one of my kids has the flu, or sometimes, our guests might not resonate with the depth of Shabbat's blessing. Yet, on those magical occasions when everything aligns—when my daughters dive deep into the Shabbat spirit, when laughter and vibrant discussions animate the air, when one of my daughters takes the lead of our gathering, inviting everyone to share their favorite part of the week, and when each dish on our table whispers tales of heritage and creativity—I feel a spiritual vibration. It's as if the room itself pulsates with a Shabbat energy, buzzing with a raw, vulnerable love. This love—a love for each other, for Shabbat, and a reflection of God's boundless love—fills every corner of the dining room.

The Shabbat dinner transcends mere physical sustenance; it satiates the soul in a manner unrivaled. Some of the most profound moments of Eden I've encountered have unfolded around my family's table, or at a table where I've been embraced as a guest. These experiences are not just meals; rather, they are feasts for the soul. The prophet Isaiah instructs the Israelite people that they should call Shabbat "*oneg*," which also means delight (Isa 58:13). For when you do, he says, you will be like "an overflowing garden" (Isa 58:11). My Shabbat dinner table is, indeed, my sacred oasis, the place where I am able to visit the garden of Eden. Such moments are, I admit, rare, yet when everyone at the table truly embodies "*hineini*"—signifying profound presence and engagement—it feels as though we've stepped into the garden. We cannot simply create these Eden moments, but Shabbat offers us a path to walk in Eden's direction. In these instances, there's no greater joy in my life.

Eden exists both nowhere and everywhere. We find it in meaningful moments not places. Before we can find our Eden, we might begin with the question "*Ayekah*?"—Where are you now? Only then can we begin to cultivate a garden of delight.

CAN YOU REALIZE YOU'RE AT THE GARDEN IN REAL TIME?

Adam and Eve are not the only people in the Bible to dwell in the garden of Eden; they were simply the first. While the Bible doesn't specifically reference anyone else ever visiting Eden, the text offers us clues to moments of Eden throughout biblical literature. One of the key words central to understanding Eden appears as Adam and Eve are expelled from the garden.

> God drove out Adam and placed him east of the garden of Eden. To protect the way to the Tree of Life, two cherubim *(kruvim)* and an ever-turning flaming sword (*cherev*) [were placed there]. (Gen 3:24)

The word for "sword" in Hebrew, *cherev*, stems from the Hebrew root ח-ר-ב, and this is the first time the word is used in the Bible.[9] When a word first appears in the Bible, its usage establishes a foundation or baseline for how we understand this word in future occurrences. Scholars call this concept "the law of first mention."[10] The initial usage sets the tone and provides key contextual clues that shape the understanding and interpretation of the word as it appears throughout the rest of the Bible. When the root of the word *cherev* (ח-ר-ב) appears in the name of a place later in the Bible, our mind should connect the name of the place with the entrance to

9. חֹרֶב can also refer to dryness or a drought. חָרְבָּה can refer to waste, desolation, or destruction.

10. Phillips, *Bible Explorer's Guide*, 127–28.

the garden of Eden. While it may seem intuitive to assume that a sword would be placed at Eden's entrance as a deterrent, the symbolism of the fiery sword tells a different tale. Remarkably, Eden is devoid of walls, fences, or any form of obstruction. Rather than serving as a barrier, it acts as a beacon, signaling the proximity of Eden's entrance, inviting all those who see it to enter. There exists solely an entrance to Eden, accessible from numerous directions.

This becomes evident when Moses shepherds his father-in-law Jethro's flock in the wilderness and arrives at a place named *Choreva*. Etymologically, we should understand this as the place of the sword. It might seem at first like a coincidence of names between *cherev* and *Choreva*, but the connection to Eden becomes significantly more obvious.

> A divine messenger from YHWH appeared to him as a blade of fire from the midst of the bush. He saw that the bush was burning with fire, but the bush was not consumed. (Exod 3:2)

Where else do we find a continuously burning blade (*labbah*) of fire that is never consumed? The answer, of course, is Eden. Like the burning bush, the ever-turning fiery sword that stands at the entrance never extinguishes (Gen 3:24).

The second clue indicating Moses is standing at the entrance to Eden originates from the detail that it's an angel, or divine messenger, who speaks to him from the burning bush. Contrary to expectations of a direct divine call, the narrative specifies it is a divine messenger who first calls out to Moses. God's direct communication with Moses is mentioned only a couple verses later (Exod 3:4). This introduction of a divine figure connects us to the cherubim, childlike angels or messengers, stationed at Eden's entrance. Cherubim, as we learn later on, rest atop the ark of the covenant and serve as a medium for God's communication (Num 7:89). Encountering cherubim, or any angelic figures of any kind, hints at being at Eden's threshold. Later, when Joshua, Moses' successor, encounters a divine messenger with a drawn sword, it signals a recurrence of the Eden motif (Josh 5:13). The divine messenger delivers the same message to both Moses and Joshua: "Remove your sandals from your feet, for the ground you are standing on is holy" (Josh 5:15; Exod 3:5). In other words, "You are in Eden, you are in the presence of God, and you know it!"

One would assume that Moses, standing in such a remarkable place, would quickly recognize its uniqueness. This phenomenon would surely captivate anyone fortunate enough to witness it. But perhaps not. Rabbi Lawrence Kushner, in his book *God Was in this Place and I Did Not Know*, poses an essential question: "How long would you have to watch wood burn before you could know whether or not it actually was being consumed?"[11] Even dried twigs would take several minutes to be consumed by a fire. At the very least, Moses would have needed to witness what could initially appear as an ordinary brush fire for several minutes to realize the extraordinary nature of the sight before him. While many individuals might have continued on their way, Moses declares, "Let me turn aside that I may see this great sight." He then proceeds to ponder the question: "Why is this bush not being burnt up?" (Exod 3:3). The reason why God chooses to speak to Moses is explicitly stated as "YHWH saw that he turned aside to see" (Exod 3:4). In that defining moment, Moses stands before the burning bush, his curiosity kindling a spark within. He witnesses what he knows cannot be, yet he does not attempt to rationalize it. Instead, he allows it to inspire him and guide his steps forward.

Moses stands at the entrance to the garden of Eden and appreciates in real time the blessings this experience holds. This narrative here reminds us that more so than any worldly pleasure, the most profound delight one can experience is through encountering God. While Moses felt a confluence of emotions including, awe, wonder, doubt, and even inadequacy, he stands at the entrance to the garden of delight and becomes transformed by it. Eden isn't a destination that we can travel to; it reveals itself as episodic glimpses of unadulterated delight that have the capacity to revolutionize our very being. The question is: Can you recognize when you are in a moment of Eden?

11. Kushner, *God Was in This Place.*

MOMENTING

There are often words in Hebrew that lack an adequate translation in English. Certain concepts in foreign languages cannot even be understood by an English-speaking culture. In Hebrew, for example, the word *firgun* (פירגון) means to take pleasure in someone else's joy or good fortune. English only has the opposite of *firgun*, which is schadenfreude, taking joy in someone else's downfall or pain. Translations of the Bible, for this reason, generally lack the nuances of some of the most powerful and transformative words and concepts found in our ancient corpus of wisdom. To fill this void, allow me to introduce a word into the English lexicon to translate an often glossed over-verse from the book of Genesis.

After Pharaoh, king of Egypt, awakens from a series of profound dreams, we learn:

וַיְהִי בַבֹּקֶר וַתִּפָּעֶם רוּחוֹ

> So it was in the morning that Pharaoh's spirit was *momenting.* (Gen 41:8)

Translators often neglect the significance of the word *va'tipaem*, and render the text "his spirit was stirred up" (Fox, *Five Books of Moses*); "his heart pounded" (Alter, *Five Books of Moses*); or "his spirit was troubled" (KJV). The root of the word *va'tipaem* (פ–ע–ם) possesses several possible meanings depending on the context. The word can mean "to beat" like a heart, as Robert Alter believes it does in this instance.[12] Yet it can also indicate a moment of time in regard to an instance or an occurrence. The latter reading would suggest that we have here a verb form of experiencing time or, as my novel translation suggests, "to moment in time." This translation aligns with the way Israelis use this verb in modern Hebrew today. It is often employed to express an intense emotional experience tied to a singular moment in time—one so powerful it feels as though it takes your breath away or intensifies your פְּעִימוֹת (p'imut), your heartbeat.

12. Alter, *Five Books of Moses*, 231.

Momenting occurs when we become aware of the sacred and holy time we are presently experiencing. Pharaoh realized that his dream was unlike normal dreams; it held a profound significance, yet he was unsure of its meaning. To unlock the dream's meaning, Pharaoh summoned all his magicians and wise men. In a lengthy process, each failed one after the other to help Pharaoh. The chief cupbearer finally suggests Joseph, a dream interpreter imprisoned at the time, who could provide insights. Consider the substantial time and effort it then took to retrieve Joseph from prison, clean him up, and present him before Pharaoh. Despite the time it took, Pharaoh remained resolute in his pursuit to understand the dream's life-changing message. Much like Moses, who stopped to perceive holiness in what others might have dismissed as an ordinary brush fire, Pharaoh paused to unravel the significance of this experience. Can you do the same? The Babylonian king Nebuchadnezzar similarly has an uncanny dream about a millennium after Pharaoh (Dan 2:1). Again, *va'tipaem rucho*—his soul was momenting; he couldn't figure out the significance of his dream, only that it grasped his spirit. Rashi (Rabbi Shlomo Yitzhaki), the 11th-century French commentator on the Bible, makes the connection that when this feeling occurs, it's as if bells *pa'amonim* are alerting us to the magnitude of the moment.[13]

When Moses encounters the bush ablaze and realizes the mystical nature of the experience, he demonstrates the sacred act of momenting. That is, Moses understands in real time that he is encountering something divine and transformational. He walks into the garden of Eden, and he knows exactly where he is. Frequently, we grasp the true importance of a sacred encounter only in hindsight. But can we, like Moses, pause and perceive the spiritual essence of a moment as it unfolds? By doing so, we not only forge enduring memories but also undergo profound transformations that positively shape our lives.

I have shared this concept with others during my teachings, and I often ask students to recall moments in their lives when they

13. Rashi on Gen 41:8, s.v. *va-tippa'em rucho*: "Like bells (*pa'amonim*) striking and clanging against one another."

have experienced "momenting." One woman vividly described the birth of her children and the indescribable feeling she had when she first laid eyes on her first daughter. Another man recounted standing beneath the wedding canopy, feeling the touch of his wife's hand as he placed the ring on her finger. Another person responded that when they are praying and everything around them seems to fade into the background, they feel that sense of momenting. In fact, the talmudic sage Reish Lakish describes a similar experience. He teaches that "one who answers amen with all his strength, they open the gates of the Garden of Eden before him" (Shabbat 119b). In other words, when we enter a flow state within our prayer, time becomes sacred time, and the space around us transforms into Eden.

Personally, I have numerous sacred memories of such moments, but nothing has ever compared to my ordination ceremony, the day I became a rabbi. I stood before the ark at Temple Emanu-El in New York City with Rabbi David Ellenson (of blessed memory), the president of my seminary, placing his hands upon my head and conferring upon me the title of rabbi. He entrusted me with the sacred duty of being a *Marbitz Torah* (spreader of Torah knowledge). Following him, my father, Rabbi Stephen Franklin, blessed me in the very same spot. I remember being overwhelmed with emotion to the point of tears and trembling. In that moment, I was not merely standing in a synagogue; it felt as if I was standing at the entrance to the garden of Eden. For me, that was the epitome of "momenting."

The experience of "momenting" is deeply personal and can vary for each individual, yet its essence remains constant—an awakening to the sacredness and transformative potential of a particular moment. Momenting is not limited to a specific context or timeframe. It transcends religious, cultural, and personal boundaries. In a world where some concepts defy adequate translation, "momenting" offers a bridge, enabling us to grasp the depth and richness of these sacred experiences.

DON'T MISS THE MOMENT

A story is told in the midrash about the sacred moment that the Israelites witnessed the greatest miracle of their generation. Fleeing Egypt and the pursuing Egyptian army, the Israelites come to the Sea of Reeds. Through the hand of Moses, God parts the sea, and the Israelites walk through walls of water on either side of them. What did the Israelites see?

Enter Reuben and Shimon, two Israelites who had been enslaved their whole lives and had only recently tasted freedom for the first time. We might forget that slaves are so accustomed to looking down that they too often fail to see what is right before them. When Shimon and Reuben march through the parted sea, all they see is mud. Reuben says to Shimon: "In Egypt, we had mud, and here at the sea, we have mud. In Egypt, we had bricks, and here we have waters stirred up like mud" (Shemot Rabbah 24:1). If only they would pick up their heads, they would see the wonder of a split sea. Instead, they only see mud.

I wonder how often we miss the miracles and blessings that are right before us. Upon further inspection, we might see Reuben and Shimon having missed a lot more than simply a marvelous sight. When the text of the Bible describes the land that they walked on, it at first calls it: "*yabasha*," dry land. God says to Moses:

> וְאַתָּה הָרֵם אֶת־מַטְּךָ וּנְטֵה אֶת־יָדְךָ עַל־הַיָּם וּבְקָעֵהוּ וְיָבֹאוּ בְנֵי־
> יִשְׂרָאֵל בְּתוֹךְ הַיָּם בַּיַּבָּשָׁה׃
>
> You, lift up your staff, and extend your hand over the sea and split it so that the Israelites can go amidst the sea on dry land. (Exod 14:16)

But when Moses actually does part the sea, the word for "dry land" changes.

> וַיֵּט מֹשֶׁה אֶת־יָדוֹ עַל־הַיָּם וַיּוֹלֶךְ יְהוָה אֶת־הַיָּם בְּרוּחַ קָדִים עַזָּה
> כָּל־הַלַּיְלָה וַיָּשֶׂם אֶת־הַיָּם לֶחָרָבָה וַיִּבָּקְעוּ הַמָּיִם
>
> Moses extended his hand and YHWH caused a strong easterly wind to blow all night, thus turning the sea into *Chorevah*, the waters were thus split. (Exod 14:21)

The Israelites aren't marching through mud or even firm dry land; if they can appreciate the moment, if they can relish the awe of the waters, if they can realize all that God is doing for them, they realize that they are walking in the very same place where Moses first encounters God—*Choreivah*, at the edge of Eden. Moses recognizes in real time that he is standing in a sacred moment in time and space, but many of the Israelites, like Reuben and Shimon, miss it altogether. And this isn't the last time they will dwell at the edge of the garden, for Sinai—the place of revelation—is only a few days' journey ahead. Perhaps not so coincidentally, the alias for Sinai used throughout the Bible, is—you guessed it—Chorev(ah).

The rabbis teach in a *midrash*, an interpretive commentary, that Mt. Sinai has six names: Sinai, Mt. Bashan, Mountain of God, Mt. Gavnunim (peaks), Mt. Chamad (desire), and Mt. Chorev. "Why was it called Mt. Chorev?" ask the rabbis. "Because there the sword is unsheathed" (Tanchuma BaMidbar 7:1). Or in other words, the ever-turning sword marks the entrance to the gate of Eden when the Israelites stand at the foot of Sinai.

The Israelites are presented with an unparalleled opportunity to reenter the garden of Eden—not physically but spiritually. Just as the garden is a space where humanity can experience delight and encounter God, so Sinai becomes hallowed ground for the Israelites to experience the Divine and receive Torah. Moses has already tasted Eden at Chorev with the burning bush, but now the entirety of the Israelite people have their chance. It is hard to miss the unsubtle moment as lightning and thunder rock the heavens and the piercing sound of the shofar grows louder and louder. At Mt. Sinai, God gives the Israelites the Torah—the very key they need to cross the threshold into Eden.

The great Jewish novelist Chaim Potok captures a glimpse of this idea in his book *The Promise*, the sequel to his most famous work, *The Chosen*. In *The Promise*, the protagonist Reuven Malter, a rabbinical student, often studies Torah with his father, David Malter, acclaimed scholar of the Talmud (a text of discussions, interpretations, and elaborations of the Torah from early rabbis). One Shabbat morning, while the two of them are off in the countryside, Reuven and his father David study together. Each regularly studies Torah as a part of their Jewish practice, but their love of Torah learning extends far beyond a simple requirement to do so. After a session of deep Torah learning together, Reuven heads out into the fields:

> I took a blanket out to the back lawn and lay in the sun . . . . Clouds drifted overhead, huge balls of white cotton moving against the brilliant blue of the sky. A cardinal disappeared into the maple and for a while it seemed the leaves were singing. I fell asleep on the blanket in the sun. I thought I heard a deep voice call my name. I opened my eyes. The grass shivered faintly in the warm breeze. I was alone on the lawn.[14]

I've always been struck by this passage. The experience goes beyond the simple mystique of nature around him. What does Reuven hear? Is it simply his imagination? Perhaps Reuven's experience is an echoing of Moses' experience at the bush that lies at the edge of Eden. "God called to him from amidst the bush and said Moses! Moses!" (Exod 3:4). Reuven's experience with Torah has appeared to have led him to the garden, where God calls out to him. Reuven seemingly thinks he imagined the deep voice, but he cannot ignore the sense of divine presence in that moment, much like Moses standing before the burning bush. It's as if the act of studying Torah has transported him to the threshold of Eden, where the boundaries between the mundane and the sacred blur.

In these moments of "momenting," whether it's Moses before the burning bush, the Israelites at the split sea, or Reuven in the peaceful countryside, there is a recognition of the extraordinary within what others see only as ordinary. These instances remind us that the sacred is all around us, waiting to be noticed and appreciated. It's a call to mindfulness, an invitation to see the world with new eyes.

So, can you realize when you're at the garden in real time? Can you recognize those moments of "momenting" in your own life? They may not always come with blazing bushes or parted

14. Potok, *Promise*, 370.

seas, but they carry the potential to transform your perception and deepen your connection with the Divine. Don't miss the moment; embrace it, cherish it, and let it lead you to your own sacred encounters.

QUESTIONS FOR CONSIDERATION:

1. **Adam's Response:** What does Adam's response to God reveal about human nature and our tendency to avoid accountability or confrontation with our shortcomings?
2. **The Concept of *Hineini*:** How does the concept of *hineini* (being present and ready) contrast with Adam's reaction in the garden of Eden, and what can we learn from this contrast?
3. **The Concept of "Momenting" in Scripture and Life:** How does the introduction of the concept of "momenting" enhance our understanding of significant spiritual experiences in both biblical stories and modern life?
4. **Where Is Your Eden?** Reflecting on the concept of Eden as more than just a physical location but as a state of emotional and spiritual fulfillment, where have you found your Eden?

2

Standing at Sinai

THERE'S A CLASSIC, PERHAPS esoterically Jewish joke that goes something like this:

> A man walks into a synagogue and sees a familiar woman, though he can't place where he knows her. "Excuse me," he says, "I know you from somewhere!"
>
> "Did you go to Jewish summer camp?" she asks.
>
> "No," replies the man.
>
> Trying to figure out where they had met, the man continues, "Did you grow up at Temple Israel?"
>
> "No," replies the woman.
>
> Suddenly, the man's eyes light up as he realizes the connection. "I know," he says, "I stood next to you at Mount Sinai!"

This joke might not seem funny unless you're a theological insider. But once you experience Sinai for yourself, you'll understand.

Mount Sinai is the sacred place where, according to the Bible, God gave the Torah (the first five books of the Hebrew Bible) to Moses and the Israelite people. In an awe-inspiring scene filled with divine phenomena—billowing smoke, blazing fire, quaking earth, roaring thunder, and flashing lightning—the Israelites bear witness to the marvels of God's presence. Amid this overwhelming spectacle, they experienced a revelation that transcended ordinary perception. The intensity of the moment created what we might call "Sinai Synesthesia"—a sensory overload so profound that it transformed the way they processed the world. At the foot of the mountain, the Israelites encountered the extraordinary: they *see sound.*

וְכָל־הָעָם רֹאִים אֶת־הַקּוֹלֹת . . . וְאֵת קוֹל הַשֹּׁפָר

> The entire people were seeing the voices . . . and the sound of the horn. (Exod 20:15)

What do sounds look like? This moment evokes a scientifically documented phenomenon called *chromesthesia*, in which specific sounds are perceived as colors—like a spiritual melody evoking swirling blues and whites. But Sinai Synesthesia may have extended beyond visualizing sound. In *lexical-gustatory synesthesia*, for example, certain words or sounds evoke distinct tastes, echoing the oft-used Jewish description of Torah tasting like sweet honey. In these moments of sensory transcendence, the world as we know it shifts; time moves differently, and we see ourselves and the universe through radically new and transformative lenses.

We might begin to understand the Sinai experience by delving into the arena of metaphysical time before exploring metaphysical space. Metaphysical time refers to a concept of time beyond the physical or quantifiable aspects of time as we generally understand it. Unlike chronological time, which is linear and measured, metaphysical time is more abstract and relates to the nature of existence, consciousness, and the universe itself. It encompasses ideas of eternity, the infinite, and the cyclical nature of time, where past, present, and future might be intertwined or experienced simultaneously. In metaphysical time, the boundaries between moments blur, allowing for a spiritual understanding of events beyond the limitations of scientific chronology. The ancient Greeks articulated this distinction by identifying two kinds of time: *chronos* and *kairos*. *Chronos* refers to measurable, sequential time—the ticking of a clock or the turning of a calendar. In contrast, *kairos* is qualitative time, representing the opportune, significant, or sacred moment when something profound unfolds. While *chronos* marks duration, kairos captures meaning, emphasizing the depth of the present moment or its transformative potential.

The rabbis of the Talmud recognized that the Torah often operates in this metaphysical, kairos-like dimension. They articulated this through the principle אין מוקדם ואין מאוחר בתורה—"there is no earlier or later in the Torah." This suggests that the Torah does not adhere to a strict, linear chronology; instead, its narrative flows in a mystical spiral, overlapping, repeating, and reinterpreting itself. Events in the Torah are not bound by temporal constraints but are instead layered and interconnected, offering a timeless, spiritual resonance that allows us to experience Sinai not as a singular historical moment but as an eternal, ongoing encounter.

We're so accustomed to measuring time in seconds, minutes, hours, and days that it's difficult to grasp metaphysical time as an abstract concept. Physicists, however, might find it easier to understand time as something relative. After all, Einstein taught us that time is shaped by two key forces: relative velocity and gravitational pull. In a phenomenon known as time dilation, the faster someone moves in relation to the speed of light, the slower time progresses for them. Likewise, in a stronger gravitational field, time also slows down. A practical example of this is with GPS satellites, which guide us with turn-by-turn directions. Because these satellites orbit in an environment with a different gravitational force than Earth, they must account for gravitational time dilation to accurately calculate our location.[1]

When exploring the scientific phenomenon of black holes, we see an even more intense parallel to metaphysical time. A black hole can be thought of as a physical manifestation of time

1. GPS satellites orbit Earth at an altitude of roughly 20,200 kilometers (12,550 miles) and experience two opposing relativistic effects: because they move at about 14,000 km/h (8,700 mph), special relativity causes their onboard clocks to run about 7 microseconds per day slower than clocks on Earth's surface; however, due to weaker gravity at their altitude, general relativity makes their clocks run about 45 microseconds per day faster. The net effect is that satellite clocks gain approximately 38 microseconds per day relative to Earth-bound clocks—an error that would accumulate to several miles of navigational inaccuracy each day if not corrected. Ashby, "Relativity in the Global Positioning System."

folding—where the fabric of time itself loops or spirals in ways that defy linear logic. In the realm of physics, black holes are places where the gravitational pull is so strong that it warps both space and time to extreme degrees. Near a black hole, time behaves in ways that are radically different from our everyday experience—it can slow down dramatically, and at the event horizon, where gravity approaches infinity, time as we know it appears to stop. This behavior of time near a black hole is not unlike the concept of metaphysical time. Just as relativity shows that time can bend and stretch in extreme gravitational environments, metaphysical time suggests that in spiritual moments, like the giving of the Torah at Sinai, time can fold in on itself, blurring the distinction between past, present, and future. In both cases, time is no longer a simple, linear progression. Here, we see that spirituality and science may not be all that dissimilar, as both realms reveal that under extraordinary conditions—whether the immense gravity of a black hole or the divine presence at Sinai—time behaves in ways that defy conventional standards of any normal clock or watch.

This understanding of time as layered and ever-present, rather than fixed in the past, is central to Jewish belief. The revelation at Sinai, for instance, didn't happen just once; it continuously unfolds in the daily lives of Jewish people. When Jews read from a Torah scroll—the sacred handwritten copy of the first five books of the Hebrew Bible—we say a blessing that calls attention to the continuous unfolding events of revelation. Within the blessing, we say the words, "We bless You YHWH, who is giving us the Torah." Note the tense of the verb "to give." It would seemingly make the most sense to say "who has given us the Torah." But using the present tense of the verb reminds the congregation that reading from the Torah is not just a remembrance but an active experience of the revelation at Sinai in the present moment. Rabbi Menachem of Kotzk asked the question "why do we mark the giving of Torah but never use the language of receiving the Torah?" He explains, "The giving of Torah took place in a fixed time, but the receiving of Torah takes place every day."[2] This idea of continuous revela-

2. Agnon, *Present at Sinai*, 216.

tion plays out in the very text of the Torah. In one of Moses' final speeches to the Israelites before they cross into the promised land, Moses tells the Israelites that the experience of revelation and covenant is for "all those who are here, and all those who are not here" (Deut 29:14). What can it mean that the revelation occurred with people who were not there? One interpretation from Rabbi Shmuel Bar Nahmani teaches that even though the bodies of future generations of Jews hadn't yet been created, their souls indeed had witnessed the events of the past (Midrash Tanchuma, Netzavim 3:1). But it seems more likely to mean that the experience of Sinai exists in metaphysical time, allowing every past, present, and future generations to partake in it.

WHERE IS SINAI?

While we have addressed the question "when was Sinai?," we still have to address "where is Mount Sinai?" Scholars have tirelessly debated this question. There are no fewer than a dozen proposed locations that people believe to be the place where God gave Moses and the Israelite people the Torah. The Monastery of Saint Catherine, an ancient and revered Christian monastery, is situated at the foot of one of the proposed locations of Mount Sinai in the Sinai Peninsula of Egypt. When you type "Mount Sinai" into Google Maps, you'll be taken to this site, called "Jabal Mousa" (Mountain of Moses) in Arabic. This historic place, dating back to the 6th century CE, is believed by many to be the original location of Sinai. The monastery is a UNESCO World Heritage site and one of the oldest continuously functioning Christian monasteries in the world. It houses an extensive collection of early Christian manuscripts and icons, second only to the Vatican in importance. Yet two thousand years separate the construction of the monastery and the revelation at Mt. Sinai, and those who understand the intricacy of the "saw you at Sinai" humor understand that many of the biblical site names need not correspond with physical places, even though we're able to find them in our lifescape.

The task of plotting Sinai on a map falls victim to the same problem we have with trying to find Eden. The clues the text offers us simply don't point to a singular place. Mount Sinai, also called *Chorev*, first appears as the place where Moses encounters God at the burning bush (*s'neh*), which would be in Midian, not the Sinai desert (Exod 3). There are those that highlight the volcanic activity at Sinai correlating to certain active volcanoes in northwest Arabia. And then there is the mention of Mount Sinai being an eleven-day-journey towards Kadesh-Barnea, which would likely place Mount Sinai somewhere in the southern Sinai desert. These places also lack proximity to any possible location of the mysterious Sea of Reeds, which would also have been a few days' journey from Mount Sinai. Some academics place Sinai in the northwestern part of the Sinai Peninsula, hypothesizing it in close proximity to the Red Sea and the Great Bitter Lake, both locations often proposed as the "Sea of Reeds." Each clue places us in a different part of the geographic map, confounding those who seek a locative location of Sinai. What they fail to see is that we cannot plot Sinai on a map, only within our life's journey.

Dr. Moshe Berhab learned this lesson when he traveled to what he thought was the real Mount Sinai in 1956. That fall, the Egyptian government had nationalized the Suez Canal and blocked cargo ships from Western countries, as well as Israel, from utilizing this essential international trade route. Israel, in a daring operation backed by both Britain and France, sent in troops to capture the area and reopen access. They occupied Sinai for about five months before relinquishing control to a United Nations Emergency Force, which ensured the freedom of navigation through the canal. Moshe Berhab was one of the Israeli troops stationed down in Sinai during that time and had the opportunity to visit one of the sites that many believed to have been Mount Sinai. He climbed the mountain with anticipation of having a spiritual experience. 3500 years before him, Moses, his namesake, had ascended the very same place and received the Torah from God. Surely he would have some kind of Sinai moment, which, we read, our ancestors had when they stood at Sinai's foot. To his disappointment, he felt nothing. He thought that perhaps the real Mount Sinai was one of the other proposed locations. When he was back home, he sent a letter to Rabbi Menachem Schneerson, the Rebbe (or spiritual leader) of the Chabad-Lubavitch movement to gain some insight on his experience, or lack thereof, at "Mount Sinai." Not surprisingly, the Rebbe does not weigh in on whether Moshe had gone to the correct location. "The significance of Sinai is not the geographic location," noted the Rebbe. Rather, "it's that the Torah was received there."[3] The Rebbe suggests that Sinai isn't a relevant location at all. Perhaps though, he simply meant that geographic Sinai isn't at all relevant. The experience of Sinai through Torah, however, enters the consciousness of the Jewish people whenever and wherever we bring Torah into our lives.

Rabbi Jason Miller shared a profound experience of feeling divine revelation at Sinai during a Shavuot celebration at his local synagogue. Shavuot, in Jewish tradition, is the Jewish holiday that commemorates the giving of the Torah at Mount Sinai, forty-nine days after the Israelites' exodus from Egypt. One hallmark of the holiday is the Tikkun Leil Shavuot, an all-night study session in which Jews immerse themselves in the wisdom of the Torah. At the end of a night-long learning marathon, the synagogue where Rabbi Miller served as a youth advisor in Metro Detroit held a special early morning service outdoors, featuring a Torah reading in the dawn light. Rabbi Miller recounts:

> It was a memorable night with many opportunities for Torah study with several wonderful teachers. With delicious snacks and caffeinated beverages, about 30 of us managed to stay up the entire night. At around 5 in the morning, we convened outside in the courtyard to enjoy the sunrise while we prayed.[4]

What followed was a moment of revelation that stayed with him. As the Torah was taken from the ark and carried around the courtyard, Rabbi Miller felt transported to Sinai itself. He recalls, "I had

3. Schneerson, "Iggeret Kodesh."

4. Miller, "Shavuot."

the sense that we really were at Mount Sinai, claiming what God had lovingly gifted to us." The connection deepened as the Torah reading seemed to echo the unfolding scene. As the reader chanted, "*On the third day, as morning dawned, there was thunder and lightning*," the weather mirrored the narrative. The sky darkened and a thunderstorm erupted. Rain poured down, and the service had to move indoors. Far from dampening the moment, the storm heightened its impact, creating what Rabbi Miller describes as his "Sinai moment." He reflected:

> I remember thinking, this must be what divine revelation feels like. It was the epitome of holiness—an existential experience full of awe and majesty, thunderclaps, and lightning bolts. Best of all, it was shared with the community. Being shaken by the thunder, seeing the lightning, and hearing the words of Torah convinced me that I really did stand at Mount Sinai. We were all there together.[5]

This story underscores a powerful lesson: experiencing Sinai is not bound by physical location or time. While sacred moments like Shavuot can bring the Sinai experience into sharper focus, the mountain can manifest anywhere and at any moment.

Jewish tradition does not glorify the place from which Torah was given, because Torah can come from any place. This is perhaps why the prophet Isaiah offers one of the most nonsensical statements about the Torah: "The Torah comes forth from Zion, and the word of God from Jerusalem" (Isa 2:3). Our first inclination is to call out, "Wrong mountain!" Mount Zion, the site upon which the Temple of Jerusalem was built, sits nowhere near Mount Sinai, nor have the two places ever been linked. But to the Rebbe's point, we discover Torah in whatever place we experience it most profoundly. In Isaiah's time, Jerusalem became the central place of Jewish spirituality. King Solomon had built a great edifice of worship and communal gathering upon Mount Zion, and that had become the locus of Jewish life. Mount Zion became Mount Sinai in Isaiah's day. Yet after Jews had been exiled from Judea to

5. Miller, "Shavuot."

Babylonia, and the heart of Jewish life developed in this foreign land, Rabbi Nathan, a Babylonian sage, paraphrased, "Out of Babylonia comes Torah, and the word of God from Nahar-Peqod" (Jerusalem Talmud, Sanhedrin 1:2:33). It was in Nahar Peqod that Rabbi Hanina had established both the central house of learning as well as the Sanhedrin, the governing body of seventy rabbis who ruled on Jewish law. We need not even find the closest mountain to bring Sinai into our lives. Sinai is simply the place where Torah is revealed before us, wherever that might be.

The Rabbinic sage Rabbi Bar Bar Ḥana learns this lesson in a story recounted in the Talmud. As he journeys through the wilderness, he is guided by an Arab who knows the sites where the Israelites experience miracles during their desert wanderings. Along the way, the guide leads him to the graves of those who perish during the forty years in the wilderness. The Arab then says to him, "Come, I will show you Mount Sinai." You can imagine Rabbi Bar Bar Ḥana's excitement, only for it to turn to dismay upon arrival. The mountain, once sacred, is now infested with scorpions the size of white donkeys, a vivid image of desolation engulfing the once-holy place. The divine voice that calls to them from that place isn't one of revelation but of lamentation (Bava Batra 74a).

This story reminds us that the physical location of Sinai is less significant than the experience of Sinai, which comes through the Torah. The giant scorpions around the desolate mountain symbolize a place stripped of its original sanctity. The once awe-inspiring mountain where the Torah was given had become a perilous place, where the shadow of death now loomed. We don't need to be at the historical location of Sinai to have a revelatory experience. Instead, we need to be at the metaphysical Sinai—the spiritual state of revelation that occurs during moments of profound encounter with the Torah and its wisdom.

MOUNTAIN MOMENTS

There are certain moments of profound learning in life where we become radically transfixed by an idea or gem of wisdom. Often, as I study biblical texts, I encounter a verse, or even a single word, that captures my spiritual imagination and induces a learning trance. In these moments, the words leap off the page and stay with me as a life guide. My colleague Rabbi Alicia Magal shared with me that she calls these experiences "mountain moments." A mountain moment is a time of revelatory learning or epiphany that sticks with you and changes the way you understand yourself and the world. In other words, it's a learning experience so profound that it transports you to the foot of Sinai.

When Rabbi Magal had been studying to become a rabbi, she had attended a week-long prayer leader's retreat, a gathering centered on developing how rabbis could observe, support, and elevate energy patterns within a prayer service. She had spent many hours meditating and praying with a supportive cohort, which all culminated for her when she was tasked with reading from the Torah, the sacred handwritten Jewish scroll that contains the first five books of the Hebrew Bible. The section of the week contained the narrative of the Israelites standing at the foot of Mount Sinai, as well as the oration of the Ten Commandments. While reading from the section about the Israelites standing at the foot of the mountain, Rabbi Magal had what she later came to describe as a "mountain moment." She had a realization that:

> Maybe there was no *physical* mountain! The people become as a mountain. They were raised up through an elevated state to a divine encounter with God, with the thunderous yet overpoweringly intimate voice echoing in each person. The Israelites rose to the height they could manage, the elders somewhat higher, the priests even higher, Aaron yet higher, and Moses to the pinnacle of what men could attain and remain alive in this world.[6]

For Rabbi Magal, this moment of revelation connected her more deeply not just to the text but with God. From this experience of divine encounter through text, she felt transported to the foot of Sinai, leading her to reflect on the paradigm of this experience through the words "mountain moments."

6. Magal, "Mountain Moment," 2.

One of my own mountain moments came while studying the very same text that Rabbi Magal was reading from when her flash of revelation occurred. I was studying Exodus 19, about the experience of revelation at Sinai, and a single word that I had read hundreds of time previously suddenly popped off the page for me. The text notes, "The Israelites encamped נגד (*neged*) the mountain" (Exod 19:2). The word *neged* in Hebrew seems quite unusual and doesn't appear all that frequently in the Hebrew Bible. It's often rendered as "across from," "in front of," "against," or "opposite." *Neged*, however, has a more complex meaning that cannot be translated with a word, as it's a larger idea. To understand this, we employ again the law of first mention and turn to Gen 2:18 to find that when God creates humanity, God establishes that it's not good for Adam to be alone. God makes Adam an "*ezer* (helper) *k'negdo*," which again suffers the same translation deficit as the above text. The word *neged* here doesn't make sense with any of its direct translations. God didn't create Eve as a helper against Adam, opposite Adam, or even in front of him. Rather, the word *neged* connotes the bringing together of two things that are seemingly different in sacred union. God makes Adam a female counterpart with whom he is brought together to complete humanity. Throughout biblical and rabbinical literature, the word *neged* functions in this vein. When the rabbis list ten of the most important acts of Jewish living—a list that includes honoring your father and your mother, assisting the bride, escorting the dead, performing acts of kindness—they conclude with the statement "the study of Torah is *neged* to them all." The study of Torah helps bring all of these beautiful acts of sacred living together in our lives. So what then does it mean to be *neged* the mountain? With a flash of revelation, I realized that the text was showing us the moment that the Israelites enjoined themselves to Mount Sinai. They forge a relationship to the mountain, carrying it with them wherever they go. I remember the very moment when I saw this connection in the text, and it was one of my many mountain moments. In this case, though, my mountain moment didn't just bring me to Mount Sinai—my mountain moment was about the very nature of my spiritual link to Mount Sinai.

The metaphysical connection of the Israelites to Mount Sinai plays out as a paradigm throughout biblical history. Later in the chronicles of the exodus from Egypt, after Moses had already descended the mountain, after Moses had smashed the first set of tablets of the covenant after witnessing the Israelites worshpping a golden calf (Exod 32), and even after the Israelites had built the tabernacle and ordained Aaron as high priest of the Israelites, we stumble upon a curious narrative in the text. "YHWH spoke to Moses on Mt. Sinai" (Lev 25:1). At this point in time, we would expect God to be speaking to Moses at the tent of meeting.[7] The Israelites had long left Mount Sinai. What is Moses doing speaking to God on Mount Sinai? When we look at the Hebrew for "on Mount Sinai," we might begin to understand the nuance of the text. God speaks to Moses בְּהַר סִינַי (*behar Sinai*). The Hebrew preposition "בְּ" or "*b'*" can mean "on," "in," or "upon," but it can also mean "with." When God speaks to Moses at this point in time, God may no longer be at Mount Sinai physically, but the experience of Sinai is with him in that moment.

We have the ability to bring Sinai with us not just wherever we go but whenever we go. Revelation occurs not just anywhere but throughout the generations of time. As Moses instructs the Israelites, the experience of covenant and revelation is for all those "who are standing here with us this day before YHWH our God, and with those who are not with us here this day" (Deut 29:14). In other words, every subsequent and successive generation will experience Sinai in their own day. We need not wander from mountain to mountain in the wilderness hoping to find Sinai; we can have mountain moments wherever and whenever. For some people, it may be as simple as being called up to read a blessing before and after the Torah is read, called an *aliyah*. For others, carrying or holding a Torah can be enough to bring them back to Sinai itself—their hands trembling with the same wonder their ancestors once felt at the mountain's base. We don't know what

7. See Exod 33:7; Lev 1:1.

our mountain moments might look like, but when they happen, recognize the potential they have to change you and your relationship with God.

QUESTIONS FOR CONSIDERATION

1. **The Concept of Metaphysical Time:** How does understanding metaphysical time, as opposed to chronological time, alter our perception of the Sinai experience and the nature of revelation?
2. **Science and Sinai:** In what ways can scientific concepts like time dilation and black holes help us understand the spiritual experience of Sinai, and how might this blend of science and spirituality deepen our understanding of Torah?
3. **Personal "Mountain Moments":** What are some of your own "mountain moments"—times when you felt profoundly connected to a sense of purpose or spirituality—and how have they impacted your relationship with Torah and God?
4. **Sinai Beyond Geography:** Jewish tradition does not tie Sinai to a specific physical location but rather emphasizes it as an experience. How does this shift in focus encourage a more accessible, personal approach to revelation?

3

The Crossroads of Haran

In the quaint village of Haran, nestled in southeastern Turkey, an intriguing phenomenon occurs among its ten thousand Turkish and Arab residents. A significant number share the names Ibrahim and Sarah, a nod to the biblical heritage deeply woven into the fabric of this ancient city, tracing back five millennia. Haran of old, perched on a hilltop some twenty miles from its modern counterpart, is imprinted in local culture and lore, its biblical significance palpable in every corner. Locals still point out the well from which Jacob, the biblical patriarch, drew water for Rachel's flock, as described in Genesis 29. Additionally, Haran's lore encompasses sites believed to have been traversed by other biblical figures, such as Adam's first garden, Jethro's (Moses' father-in-law) house, and the dwelling of Abraham's brother Haran—a namesake different in spelling from the city itself.[1]

Beyond its historical allure, modern Haran thrives as a mosaic of cultural and social activity, where the ancient traditions blend with the rhythms of contemporary life. The marketplaces buzz with activity, offering a vibrant array of local crafts, textiles, and spices. The air is perfumed with the scent of local cuisine, where

1. In Hebrew, the city Haran is spelled חרן and is pronounced *Charan*, while the name of Abraham's brother is הרן, pronounced *Haran*.

dishes passed down through generations are savored, embodying the fusion of Turkish and Arab influences. Amidst this, the town's unusual beehive-shaped houses stand as a distinctive architectural feature. This blend of ancient legacy and modern vibrancy positions Haran as a unique junction of eras, where history is not merely preserved but actively experienced each day. Haran, deriving its name from Akkadian and Hebrew, means "crossroads." It represents not only a pivotal node along ancient Near Eastern trade routes but also serves as a metaphysical crossroads, reflecting the universal journey of discovery and decision that intersects the paths of all individuals at various moments in life.

The biblical figures who wind up trekking through Haran enter not just an intersection of biblical highways; rather they find themselves at life's crossroads, stuck without a way to move forward. Terah, Abraham's father, decides to uproot his family without a given reason and travel from Ur Chasdim—an unknown location in the heart of ancient Mesopotamian civilization—to the land of Canaan, a journey of at least one thousand miles.

> Terah took his son Abram; his grandson Lot, the son of Haran; and his daughter-in-law Sarai, the wife of his son Abram, and they set out together from Ur Chasdim for the land of Canaan. (Gen 11:31)

Along the way, they arrive at the crossroads of Haran, abandon their original destination, and settle there.

Upon reaching Haran, they cease their journey, and there, Terah spends the remainder of his days until passing away at 205 years of age. The time Abraham (then known as Abram) spends in Haran is often overlooked. While the biblical text states that Terah is 70 at Abraham's birth (Gen 11:26) and 205 at his death (Gen 11:32), and Abraham was 75 when he departed Haran for Canaan, the exact duration of Abraham's stay in Haran remains unclear. However, other ancient texts provide some insights. A parabiblical fragment from the Dead Sea Scrolls suggests Abraham is seventy when leaving Ur Chasdim and stays in Haran for five years,[2]

2. 4Q252 (The 4th Cave of Qumran Fragment number 252): 8 . . . Terah

whereas the Book of Jubilees, an apocryphal text dating to the second century BCE, proposes a fifteen-year stay.[3] Whether five or fifteen years, Abraham would have left Haran while his father was still alive, leaving him behind along with his brother Nahor. Regardless of the exact time frame in Haran, his tenure there is not unsubstantial; it spans a period of his life when he got stuck.

Haran represents more than a physical crossroads in biblical narratives; it's home to where our ancestors grapple with the challenge of moving on. Abraham's prolonged stay transforms Haran from a mere stopover into a home, a place he has to be divinely urged to leave to fulfill his greater destiny. God commands Abraham to *lech lecha*—"Go forth from your native land, from your kin, from your father's house, to the land that I will show you" (Gen 12:1). This seems peculiar, given that Abraham has long left Ur Chasdim. However, his extended stay ingrains Haran into his identity, making it his new native land. Similarly, Abraham's brother Nahor remains in Haran, turning a journey's pause into a permanent settlement (Gen 24:10). This highlights Haran's seductive nature to entice and hold. The crossroads are typically understood as a place to pass through, even if we linger, but there are those who find Haran as their ultimate destination, unable to leave its grasp over us. The crossroads are typically understood as places we move through—pausing, perhaps, but not meant to remain. Abraham, aware of this danger, warns his servant Eleizer not to allow his son to be drawn back into the place they were called to leave: "Make sure that you do not ever bring my son back there" (Gen. 24:6). This directive reflects Abraham's understanding of Haran's alluring yet stagnating influence, a place of deferred dreams and destinies. It's a poignant reminder of the human tendency to linger at crossroads, comfortable in the familiar yet paralyzed by the potential of the unknown. The biblical narrative thus positions Haran

was one hundred and fo[r]ty years old when he went forth

9 from Ur of the Chaldees and entered Haran (11:31b). And Ab[ram was se]venty years old. And for five years

10 Abram stayed in Haran. cf: Genesis Rabbah 39:7

3. Jub 12:12; cf. Kato, "Ancient Chronography."

as a landmark in both physical and spiritual journeys, a snare not just for Abraham but for all who face their own Harans in life.

Abraham's concerns about Isaac visiting Haran reflect a deeper understanding of the place's mystical allure. Haran, with its rich history and familial connections, has the power to captivate and hold those who seek only to pass through. It isn't just the physical crossroads that make Haran unique but also its role as a metaphysical junction, a place where decisions about one's future and destiny are made and remade. This characteristic of Haran is mirrored in the lives of those who find themselves within its walls. Just as Abraham has to break free from its embrace to fulfill his destiny, he fears Isaac might face the same challenge. Haran is more than a waypoint; it is a test of resolve and faith. The city's legacy, therefore, is not just in its historical and biblical significance but also in its role as a place of choice and change. Abraham's journey and his directive to Eliezer underline this symbolism, marking Haran as a crucial pivot in the narrative of personal and spiritual journey, not just for Abraham but for all who follow in his footsteps.

Isaac, unlike his father, never ventures to Haran. However, his son Jacob finds himself in Haran under dramatic circumstances, fleeing from his brother Esau's death threat. He ends up spending a significant portion of his life—twenty years—in this place. Initially, it is love that anchors him there; he falls deeply in love with Rachel, his uncle Laban's daughter. To win her hand, Jacob agrees to work for Laban for seven years, but on the wedding night, Laban deceives him by substituting Leah, his eldest daughter, for Rachel. Undeterred, Jacob commits to another seven years of labor for Rachel. After marrying Rachel, Jacob's stay in Haran is extended by another six years. The first fourteen years can be attributed to his profound love for Rachel, but the remaining period is influenced by his growing wealth and prosperity under Laban's employment. Laban, recognizing the blessings that Jacob brings, persuades him to stay longer, offering a share of the flock as compensation.

It is only after two decades in Haran that Jacob experiences a divine intervention, echoing the call his grandfather Abraham once received. God speaks to Jacob, urging him to return to the land of his forefathers, the land of his birthright: "Return to the land of your ancestors, to your kin, and I will be with you" (Gen 31:3). Unable to leave of his own accord, it takes the divine voice to shake Jacob out of the comfortable life he has grown accustomed to in Haran. Jacob's protracted stay there, much like Abraham's, represents more than just a physical residence; it underscores the difficulty of leaving a place of comfort and prosperity, even when it diverts us from our destined path. Had God not called him to do so, Jacob might do the very thing that his grandfather Abraham fears for his son Isaac—he would never leave the crossroads.

THREE REASONS WE GET STUCK IN HARAN

1. Fear of the Unknown

> "The oldest and strongest emotion of mankind is fear, and the oldest and strongest kind of fear is fear of the unknown."
>
> —H. P. LOVECRAFT[4]

H. P. Lovecraft (Howard Phillips Lovecraft) was an American author known for his contributions to the genre of weird fiction and cosmic horror. He is best known for pioneering the subgenre of cosmic horror, which is characterized by the idea that there are ancient, powerful, and malevolent cosmic forces beyond human comprehension. These forces often lie dormant or hidden in the universe and can drive individuals to madness when confronted with their existence. Lovecraft's stories frequently featured these incomprehensible beings, which all played on the human primal fear of the unknown.

Modern psychologists identify fear of the unknown as the fundamental fear, "a fear that rules all other fears, brings them together producing anxiety, and binds them, facilitating anxiety and neuroticism."[5] Certain fears, like the fear of death or pain, might

4. Lovecraft, *Miscellaneous Writings*, 106.

5. Carleton, "Fear of the Unknown."

be considered fundamental, yet fear of the unknown appears even more primary; it's an inherent fear that doesn't require prior learning. Fear of the unknown also plays as one of the central reasons we get stuck in Haran.

The mentality of "the devil you know is better than the devil you don't" hinders our ability to move ourselves to a place of growth. Abraham had never been to Canaan, but he had spent a large portion of his life in Haran. What was the incentive for him to leave for a place he'd never been, and knew little about? Even for Jacob, who had grown up in Canaan, returning to Canaan might mean the blessing of reconciliation with his brother, or perhaps being killed by his brother—the feelings of his brother toward him were unknown. People often prefer dwelling in monotony rather than journeying to the frontier of possibility and encountering the risks that come along with the unknown.

The effects of uncertainty on human cognition and behavior have been explored by various behavioral economists and psychologists. Daniel Kahneman, a renowned behavioral economist and Nobel laureate, has extensively studied how humans perceive and react to uncertainty and the unknown. He suggests that people's fear of the unknown often stems from their inherent "loss aversion," a concept Kahneman and Amos Tversky introduced, which explains that people prefer avoiding losses to acquiring equivalent gains. Kahneman argues that the unknown represents a potential loss or threat in our minds, triggering a more substantial emotional response than a known entity. Unknown risks or outcomes are harder to quantify and thus can seem more threatening or concerning. Psychologist Ema Tanovic's research came to similar conclusions. She performed a series of studies where they hooked up participants to electrodes capable of delivering a harmless but slightly painful electric shock to the skin. Researchers measured the physiological responses that tend to correlate with stress—such as the sweating of the skin or changes in pupil size—and found that any element of unpredictability significantly increases people's discomfort, despite there being no objective difference in the intensity of the shock. Participants show greater stress if there is a 50 percent chance that they might receive a shock, for example, compared to situations in which there is a 100 percent certainty that they will be electrocuted. However irrational, people fear the uncertainty of whether or not they will be shocked more than the fear of the shock itself.[6]

The impact of the unknown on human psychology and behavior is substantial, leading to increased stress and avoidance of unpredictable situations. This aversion to uncertainty is deeply ingrained in human behavior and can significantly affect decision-making and daily life. It should be no surprise then, that Abraham avoided the unknown promised land of Canaan; the fright of the unknown can terrify and paralyze even the best of us. The familiarity of Haran, even when it's detrimental, can be comforting.

2. The Comforts of Haran

Langston Hughes, in his poignant poem "Harlem," wrestles with a single, piercing question: What becomes of a dream that is pushed aside, postponed, or left behind? In exploring that question, he imagines a range of possible outcomes—some painful, some unsettling, and some unexpectedly gentle. Among them is the possibility that a dream deferred doesn't always collapse dramatically; sometimes it settles into a kind of sweetness, a hardened but comforting stillness. Hughes urges us to consider that being stuck can feel, paradoxically, like a safe haven.[7]

A similar dynamic unfolds in the story of Terah and Nahor. In choosing to remain in Haran, they may never have looked back with regret. Their choice to stay, far from being a missed opportunity, might have been an unforeseen blessing. This perspective challenges the commonly held belief that relentless pursuit of a dream is always the right path. Sometimes, the greatest realization is recognizing the blessings in our current circumstances,

6. Tanovic et al., "Intolerance of Uncertainty."

7. Hughes, "Harlem," 268.

understanding that not all dreams are meant to be chased—some are destined to dissolve as we awaken to the richness of our present.

This realization prompts an essential question: Can you recognize the blessing of being in Haran? The wise Ben Zoma teaches that the person who is rich is "the person who is content with their lot" (Avot 4:1). For Abraham, Canaan is the promised land, but for Terah and Nahor, Haran may well be their destined haven.

The magnetic pull of comfort zones is powerful, and many of us find ourselves drawn to them. Some of us stay only for a while, eventually realizing that the safety and contentment of Haran might be holding us back from achieving our life's ambitions. Others choose to remain indefinitely, possibly missing out on brighter opportunities that lie beyond. Which of these resonates with you?

3. Fear of Success

In the early 1970s, psychologist Matina Horner first articulated the phenomenon of "fear of success," a concept that delves into the complex psychological landscape of human achievement. Horner's groundbreaking research, focusing on the motivational patterns among women, unveiled a startling revelation: a considerable number of female participants were entangled in a web of apprehension and adverse associations with the notion of success. This was particularly pronounced in areas predominantly male-centric or where success challenged traditional gender norms and potentially led to societal alienation or internal conflict.[8]

Over the years, this concept has transcended its initial gender-centric scope, revealing that individuals across all gender spectrums may grapple with this fear, influenced by an intricate blend of personal, societal, and psychological factors. Those harboring a fear of success might, without conscious awareness, undermine their own efforts. This self-sabotage is a defense against potential consequences such as heightened responsibilities, escalated expectations, and the erosion of privacy. This conflict manifests as an

8. Horner, "Sex Differences."

internal paradox, where the conscious desire for success is at odds with the subconscious aversion to its perceived drawbacks. While the fear of failure is a more palpable and prevalent concern, the fear of success lurks in the shadows, equally paralyzing.

Although this understanding is a relatively recent development in psychological discourse, its underlying principles are timeless. It might well be a critical factor contributing to the inertia of those dwelling in Haran, reluctant to leave. From an external vantage point, the trajectory towards success seems laden with virtues. Yet, when confronted with personal crossroads, we often retreat at the threshold of opportunity, oblivious to the psychological barriers silently eroding our resolve to embrace success.

Reflecting on the biblical narrative, this fear of success might have been the invisible shackle that held our patriarchs in Haran, hesitant to venture into the promised land. The daunting responsibilities accompanying a covenant with God, the looming expectations of greatness, and the overwhelming nature of the changes—however positive—that settlement in the promised land would impose on their lives and lineage, could very well be attributed to an underlying fear of success.

BEING SACRED CROSSERS

Rabbi David Wolpe tells the story of a time he was asked to teach a seminar for a group of rabbinical students alongside Rabbi Lawrence Kushner. They both agreed but shortly after, forgot about the commitment. A few days before the seminar was to begin, they received a phone call asking, "What's the title of the seminar?" Both hadn't given any thought to what they were going to teach about. Hurriedly, they called one another to figure out the topic of their teaching. Rabbi Wolpe was in a panic, but Rabbi Kushner calmly said, "I have a title that always works for every Jewish group, and at any time—Judaism at the Crossroads."[9]

9. Rabbi David Wolpe, remarks at Recharging Reform Judaism conference, attended by the author, May 29, 2024.

It seems that Judaism always sits at a crossroads, that we are perpetually in a state of Haran. So too, throughout the biblical narrative and throughout life, we find ourselves at sacred crossings, pivotal moments where we confront an obstacle in our path, be it a river, a bridge, or a radical exodus. These junctures pose a critical question: Can we muster the courage to cross over? We too often fail to give much thought for one of the namesakes of the ancient Israelite people, that is, the name Hebrews, or in Hebrew, *Ivrim* (עברים). The etymology comes from the Hebrew root ע-ב-ר, which means "to cross over." To be a Hebrew, in other words, means to be someone who can cross over from one side to the next.

To understand the origin of this name, we flip back to the very first person to be called a Hebrew, and that is Abraham. Amidst a chronicling of wars between Canaanite kings and the city Sodom, we learn about the kidnapping of Abraham's nephew Lot. An escapee informs Abraham—referred to as "Abraham the Hebrew"—of Lot's plight.[10] This title, "*Ivri*" (עברי), poses a question: Why was Abraham named with this epithet? The 13th-century French scholar Rabbi David Kimhi, known as Radak, suggests a link to Abraham's ancestor Eber, yet this connection seems tenuous. Another interpretation, offered by Rabbi Shlomo Yitzhaki (Rashi), drawing on Midrash, points to Abraham's geographic crossing from beyond the Euphrates River. What yields Abraham the title "the crosser" is his ability to make the sacred crossing where others could not.

God's call to Abraham—"go forth"[11]—is a summons to embark on a sacred crossing from the familiar to the unknown, from comfort to the realms of uncertainty and challenge, and most importantly, from the culture of idolatry to monotheistic faith. Abraham's legacy to his descendants becomes the capacity to undertake these sacred crossings when God, or when life, calls us to our destiny.

These sacred transitions are seldom straightforward. Consider Jacob, Abraham's grandson. Upon leaving Haran after two

10. Gen 14:13.

11. Gen 12:1.

decades, he confronts a daunting transition at the Jabbok crossing.[12] Jacob ensures the safe passage of his family and all his belongings to the opposite shore, but he remains alone on the original side of the river. "Jacob was left alone" (Gen 32:25). In his aloneness, Jacob encounters a mysterious entity with whom he struggles before he can make the crossing himself. "He struggled with a man until the break of dawn" (Gen 32:25). The key word to understand here is the word "alone." How could it be that in his aloneness, he encounters another? The answer, as many notice, is that the man with whom he struggles is none other than himself. The ambiguous grammar of the wrestling match makes it impossible to distinguish most of the subjects of verbs used throughout the conflict, suggesting that this was a battle between Jacob and self, not Jacob and another. The source of the conflict, it seems, is Jacob's fear of not only crossing back into the promised land but encountering his estranged brother, who may still harbor animus toward him.

Similarly, the story of Moses reflects the complexities of these crossings. Moses, who leads the Israelites out of Egypt into the wilderness of Sinai, prays to God to be able to cross into the promised land of Canaan (Israel).

> Please, let me cross over so that I can see the good land on the other side of the Jordan crossing. (Deut 3:25)

But God does not allow him to cross over, recounts Moses, and in a biblical pun that translates well into English, he offers that it is because "YHWH is cross with me." Moses can only be the guide who leads the Israelites to the sacred crossing at the Jordan River. He can only offer them wisdom on how they can overcome fear and anxiety for what's ahead and their nostalgia for all that they leave behind. The Israelites had wandered their way to the promised land, but at every step of the journey, they second-guess

12. The Jabbok or Yabbok River, known in Hebrew as יַבֹּק, flows into the Jordan River from the east and is situated just south of the Yarmuk River. Its Hebrew name originates from one of two possible meanings: either from a root word signifying the act of emptying or, through assonance, may be connected to Jacob's self struggle by the word יֵאָבֵק (ya'avek), to wrestle or to struggle.

their choice of leaving in the first place. They remember fondly the comforts of predictability that Egypt offers; they long for stasis. On the fortieth year of their journey, as they sit on the precipice of the promised land at the Jordan River crossing, Moses teaches them how to imagine crossing over into the next stage of their lives:

וְלֹא־מֵעֵבֶר לַיָּם הִוא לֵאמֹר מִי יַעֲבָר־לָנוּ אֶל־עֵבֶר הַיָּם

> Do not say to yourself that I cannot cross over the crossing, and that someone must cross over for me. (Deut 30:13)

Despite the trepidation of crossing into a new frontier, we journey forward. Moses emphasizes:

כִּי־קָרוֹב אֵלֶיךָ הַדָּבָר מְאֹד בְּפִיךָ וּבִלְבָבְךָ לַעֲשֹׂתוֹ

> You are already close (to crossing), so much so that you can taste it, and you can feel in your heart that you can do it. (Deut 30:14)

In essence, the biblical narrative teaches that to be a Hebrew, an *Ivri*, is to be a sacred crosser, one who dares to traverse unknown landscapes, leaving behind the comfort of the past to embrace the uncertainty of the future. Just as the Israelites evolved into Hebrews, ready to enter the promised land after forty years in the wilderness, we too are called to embrace our identity as sacred crossers, venturing forth into new chapters of our lives.

HEARING THE SACRED CALLING TO LEAVE

Once or twice in a lifetime
A man or woman may choose
A radical leaving, having heard
Lech l'cha—Go forth.
God disturbs us toward our destiny
By hard events
And by freedom's now urgent voice
Which explode and confirm who we are.

The Crossroads of Haran

We don't like leaving
But God loves becoming.

—Rabbi Norman Hirsh[13]

I embarked on my rabbinical journey as an assistant, later becoming an associate rabbi at Temple Beth Elohim in Wellesley, Massachusetts. This opportunity came after my ordination from Hebrew Union College—Jewish Institute of Religion. However, not many are aware that initially, my wife, Stephanie, hesitated to relocate to the Boston area, mere minutes from where she was raised. Despite her parents residing in nearby Newton, Massachusetts, and having a close-knit circle of friends in the neighborhood, Stephanie yearned for a new adventure, desiring to live somewhere completely new to both of us. Upon hearing my inclination to move to this area, she spent over a week in tears. My mother-in-law, Carol (may her memory be a blessing), considered me the world's best son-in-law for bringing her daughter back home. I was convinced it was the right move for us, and deep down, I think Stephanie knew it too. Eventually, Stephanie internalized the blessings of being near her family and friends. Nevertheless, after four enriching years at Temple Beth Elohim, I sensed a need to progress in my rabbinic journey. My time there might not have matched Abraham's tenure in Haran, but I felt a calling. Despite my love for the Beth Elohim community and the comfort I found in my role there, staying would limit my growth as the rabbi I aspired to become. Serving as one of four rabbis in a substantial congregation, I was content with my duties, yet I yearned for more. I realized that I was too comfortable in Haran, satisfied yet unfulfilled. A higher purpose called to me, encouraging me to seek a more significant rabbinical role elsewhere. Thus, I faced the tough decision to depart and seek a senior rabbinical position at another synagogue. The departure was both heart-wrenching and exhilarating, a necessary step in my journey. Norman Hirsh's poem on radical departure became the guiding principle through this pivotal transition.

13. Hirsh, "Shabbat Morning 1."

Particularly resonant were these lines from Rabbi Hirsh's poem: "God disturbs us toward our destiny by hard events." Often, in our efforts to rationalize trauma and adversity, we overlook their role as catalysts propelling us towards our fate. Hirsh also highlighted the dichotomy of departure and transformation, which is seldom seen in unison—"We don't like leaving but God loves becoming." Upon reflection, the contrast reveals itself as two facets of the same phenomenon. Our preoccupation with the ordeal of leaving overshadows the transformative power it holds in shaping us into who we are meant to be. What seems like a divine summons to leave is, in reality, an invitation to step into the role God has envisioned for us. Embracing this perspective eases the journey from Haran, making it a more manageable endeavor.

The shift in perspective, as inspired by Rabbi Hirsh's poem, led me to view my departure not as a loss but as a transformative journey towards fulfilling my true potential. This realization brought both clarity and strength. My dwelling in Haran symbolized a period of preparation and maturation, rather than my ultimate calling. Embracing this new chapter meant acknowledging the need for change and personal development. I began to see my leaving as an essential step in becoming the rabbi I aspired to be, one capable of impacting a community in profound and meaningful ways. This transition was more than a change in location or title; it was an evolution in my spiritual odyssey and leadership. Departing, though fraught with challenge, was a testament to my dedication to heed God's call. It was an act of faith, a trust in an unseen but promising path ahead, essential for my growth and highest service. This mindset transformed the pain of leaving into excitement for the future.

God's sacred call to us cannot be ignored despite the pain of heeding the voice. Hannah Senesh, the great Jewish poet, endured a radical departure far more intense than anything I have yet experienced in my life. She fled persecution as a Jewish woman in Hungary and captured the emotion of this life's transition in her poem "The Voice." Most of those who didn't leave suffered the fate of Auschwitz after the Hungarian Jewish population was deported in 1944, though the pain of all that was left behind was nonetheless piercing for Senesh, an anguish for all that she lost in her flight from her native land.

קוֹל קָרָא, וְהָלַכְתִּי,
הָלַכְתִּי, כִּי קָרָא הַקּוֹל.
הָלַכְתִּי לְבַל אֶפֹּל.
אַךְ עַל פָּרָשַׁת דְּרָכִים
סָתַמְתִּי אָזְנַי בַּלֹּבֶן הַקָּר
וּבָכִיתִי.
כִּי אִבַּדְתִּי דָבָר.
קיסריה 1942

A voice calls to me, and I went
I went, because the voice calls
I went to avoid falling
Yet when at the crossroads
I blocked my ears with the frost's whiteness
And I cried, for I lost something
—December 1942, Caesarea[14]

In mathematics, a net positive result is always positive—no matter how many negatives contribute to it. But in life, the equation is never that simple. Every decision we make carries its share of pain and loss, even when it moves us in a positive direction. Emigrating to Palestine may have been the best choice for Hannah Senesh but leaving home was fraught with heartbreak.

In a sad twist of irony, the poem also foreshadows another crossroads in Senesh's life. After joining the Palmach—the Jewish fighting brigade against the Nazis—she chose to parachute back into Europe to support the resistance. She was captured and ultimately killed. She was called to her mission, and despite being safe in Palestine, she once again left her life behind in answer to that call—a call to confront the very force that sought to annihilate her and her people. The voice that calls to us isn't always clear, yet when we hear it, we often have no choice but to leave behind the comforts of our own Haran, no matter how compelling they may be.

14. Szenes, "Voice Called." English translation by the author.

QUESTIONS TO CONSIDER ABOUT HARAN

1. **Personal Harans:** Reflect on a time in your life when you felt stuck in your own "Haran." What were the comforts or fears that kept you there, and how did you, or how might you, find the strength to move forward?
2. **Fear of the Unknown vs. Attraction of Stability:** How do you balance the fear of the unknown with the comfort of stability in your life decisions? Do you find yourself more often embracing change or clinging to familiarity, and why?
3. **Fear of Success:** Have you ever experienced a fear of success? How did it manifest in your life, and what steps did you take, or could you take, to overcome this fear?
4. **Sacred Crossings:** Can you identify a "sacred crossing" in your life—a pivotal moment that required you to leave behind the familiar and take a leap of faith? How did you navigate this transition, and what did you learn about yourself in the process?
5. **Hearing the Sacred Calling:** Reflect on Rabbi Norman Hirsh's words: "We don't like leaving, but God loves becoming." How does this resonate with your personal or spiritual journey? Have there been moments where you felt a "sacred calling" to evolve or transform, and how did you respond to this call?

4

Trekking Through the *Midbar*

THE STORY OF HAGAR, a pivotal yet often overlooked figure in the Bible, introduces us to the profound symbolism of the *Midbar* (wilderness). She becomes entwined in the complex dynamics of Abraham's household when his wife Sarah, unable to conceive, offers Hagar to Abraham as a surrogate to fulfill God's promise of offspring. Sarah came to despise Hagar out of her jealousy, which only grew when Hagar became pregnant. With no direction except away from the hostility, Hagar flees with nothing more than the child in her womb. In her emptiness, Hagar finds herself in the *Midbar*, and it's there that a divine messenger speaks to her and offers her a sacred question that each and every one of us is asked when we enter the holy and empty *Midbar*: "Where are you coming from, and where are you going?" (Gen 16:8). The *Midbar* is the place that we go to figure out the answer to this seemingly simple yet life-changing question. Such a question hearkens us back to the question the chief of police in Belarus asks the rabbi: "How am I to understand that God, who is omniscient, asks Adam, 'Where are you?'" Again, this is not a question about place but metaphysical space. Hagar's response, "I am a fugitive from my mistress Sarai"

(Gen 16:8), answers neither part of the question that she is asked but better responds to what Adam is asked. The question of the *Midbar* is not about "where are you in your world"; it's about figuring out your past and how it might inform your future. In the wilderness, the divine voice offers guidance, encouraging her to return for her child's sake, promising that a great nation will emerge from him. Would you, like Hagar, heed a voice that might seem at best counterintuitive or, at worst, destructive? Today's wisdom often urges, "Escape your abuser! Find the strength to leave!" If a modern-day Hagar sought my counsel, I would tell her simply, "Run—get out while you can." However, the Voice in the wilderness is not to be dismissed lightly; sacred callings may not always align with our understanding, but we should never overlook them. Perhaps she learned from Abraham the valuable lesson that when we hear the divine call, we cannot ignore it; instead, we should follow the uncomfortable and sometimes counterintuitive voice that calls us to go forward, or in Hagar's case, to go back.

Hagar's experience in the *Midbar* sets a foundational example for all who find themselves in a state of emptiness, seeking guidance and purpose. This *Midbar* experience is not just a biblical narrative; it extends to us in our lifescape, offering a space where we can hear the soft murmuring of God's voice. The *Midbar* calls us to reflect on our life's path with the poignant questions: "Where are you coming from, and where are you going?" This inquiry in our own *Midbar* moments leads us towards clarity, direction, and a deeper understanding of ourselves.

THE *MIDBAR*: THE PLACE WHERE GOD SPEAKS TO US

The Bible is no stranger to the wilderness. In fact, the majority of the Torah, the first five books of the Hebrew Bible, is set in a place betwixt Egypt and Canaan called "*Midbar*," often translated as the wilderness. The Israelites spend forty years wandering the landscape of the *Midbar* before they are able to enter the promised land. While the journey should have only taken eleven days,

God led them through this spiritual wilderness to incubate their growth from slaves to a free people, from tribes to a nation, and from the rule of Pharaoh to a nation under God and Torah. "God led the people roundabout through the *Midbar* (Wilderness)" (Exod 13:18). More than a mere geographic transition from Egypt to Israel, the *Midbar* symbolizes a profound metaphysical passage through which the Israelites forge their identity and gain spiritual enlightenment. Crucially, it is in the *Midbar* that they experience divine revelation and deepen their connection with God. The prophet Hosea eloquently portrays the *Midbar* as a sacred space of divine courtship with the Israelites, highlighting God's enduring promise despite their straying: "I will speak to her coaxingly, and lead her through the wilderness" (Hos 2:16).

The *Midbar's* significance extends beyond the Israelite journey; it is a place where God communicates with various biblical figures. God speaks to Hagar in the *Midbar* (Gen 16), is present with Joseph in the pit located in the *Midbar* (Gen 37), and appears to Moses at the burning bush in the *Midbar* (Exod 3). These instances underscore the *Midbar* as not just a physical locale but a spiritual conduit for divine communication with each of us.

The Hebrew words "*Midbar*" (מִדְבָּר) and "*medaber*" (מְדַבֵּר), though spelled the same, convey distinct yet interconnected meanings. "*Midbar*," meaning wilderness, and "*medaber*," meaning speaking, intertwine to illustrate the wilderness as a sacred space for divine communication. The *Midbar*, more than a mere physical wilderness, signifies a place of spiritual encounter where one can attune to God's voice. This concept transcends the need for a physical journey akin to that of the Israelites; the *Midbar* represents a metaphysical realm, a sanctuary free from the material world's clatter, distractions, and populace.

Unlike the cacophony and sensory overload of city life, the *Midbar* embodies a realm of profound silence and solitude. It's a place where the subtlest divine whispers can be discerned, otherwise drowned out in the tumult of civilization. This concept is poignantly illustrated in the experience of the prophet Elijah, who, in solitude in the *Midbar*, discerns the voice of God not in grandiose displays but in the "קוֹל דְּמָמָה דַקָּה—a soft murmuring voice" (1 Kgs 19:13). The *Midbar* thus emerges not merely as a void but as a richly resonant space of spiritual clarity and divine revelation, filled with a profound and meaningful murmuring of God's voice.

What does the murmuring sound like? Rabbi Alan Ullman, one of my mentors, shared with me an unforgettable experience: after a massive storm hit New England one February, he ventured out to witness the sunrise, only to find the skies overcast, less than ideal to catch the rising sun. However, what he encountered instead was a different kind of spectacle. In the aftermath of the storm, thousands of moon snail shells had been deposited along the shoreline, right where the tide recedes. With the tide silent, the air still and profoundly quiet, the only audible sound was the gentle clattering of these shells against one another. The shells, varying in size, created a symphony of unique sounds as they gently tickled each other with the tide, producing a natural percussive concert that lasted about twenty minutes. Nothing could describe the exact sound, but he imagined it would be similar to the sound of a thousand oddly shaped wind chimes. This wasn't the work of human hands; it was a breathtaking display of God's creation. Rabbi Ullman realized he was witnessing a sound so rare and extraordinary that he had never seen it captured in poetry, television, or novels. It was a simple yet miraculous event, a clear message that "God was in this place, and I didn't know it" (Gen 28:18). Although Revere Beach is accessible to approximately 1.5 million people living within a half-hour's drive, only Rabbi Ullman and a solitary wanderer he encountered were privileged to hear what he described as the murmuring of God's voice that day. Most people might never notice the divine sounds; this awareness requires a unique kind of attention to the world around us and the ability to interpret the murmuring.

Avivah Zornberg, in her book *The Murmuring Deep*, shares that when God began to create the world, the canvas for God's creation was "*tehom*" (תְּהוֹם), typically translated as "the deep," or some variation of a dark watery soup that God's words bring into existence. Zornberg suggests we might better understand *tehom* as "the murmuring deep," which captures some of the complex harmonics of the Hebrew roots: *hamam* (הָמַם), *hamah* (הָמָה), and *hom* (הוּם), offering meanings like "humming, murmuring, cooing, groaning, tumult, music, restlessness, stirring, panic."[1] This introduces a vast spectrum of tones, sounds, and movements. The murmur is not always perceived with our ears but is felt with our very essence, resonating and vibrating throughout our bodies. A question we encounter in the *Midbar* is: Can you tune into the frequency of God?

THEOPATHY—HEARING GOD IN THE STATIC

Most of us know IQ—the capacity for logical problem-solving. Many now know EQ—*emotional intelligence*—a term first defined by psychologists Peter Salovey and John D. Mayer (1990) and later popularized by Daniel Goleman (1995).[2] But the *Midbar* asks for something different: SQ—Spiritual Intelligence. If EQ is the skill of sensing another's feelings, SQ is the capacity to attune to the divine frequency within and between people. Where EQ cultivates empathy, SQ cultivates what we might call theopathy—a disciplined receptivity to the Voice that hums beneath the noise of life. The *Midbar* is the training ground for SQ—less a place you go than an environment you enter, where interference drops and reception clears.

Modern research in the field of noetic science has begun to explore a related idea known as non-local consciousness—the hypothesis that awareness is not confined to the brain but functions more like a receiver than a hard drive.[3] The mind, in this view, is a tuning instrument rather than a storage device. When we enter a *Midbar* state—quiet, still, undistracted—we open the bandwidth of the soul to receive frequencies that normally elude perception. The prophets intuited this long before neuroscience could model it: consciousness itself is spacious, and revelation arrives when the

1. Zornberg, *Murmuring Deep*, loc 234.

2. Salovey and Mayer, "Emotional Intelligence"; Goleman, *Emotional Intelligence*.

3. See Wahbeh, *Science of Channeling*; Goff, *Galileo's Error*.

self becomes still and focused enough to hear it. Theopathy, then, is not mysticism reserved for the rare few but a learnable mode of awareness. It is what Moses practiced when he turned aside to notice a bush that burned but was not consumed. It is what Elijah discovered when he realized that God's voice was not in the fire or the wind but in the soft murmuring voice. It is what Rabbi Alan Ullman heard in the rhythmic clatter of moon snail shells on the beach after the storm—a sound that most would have missed yet, for him, was unmistakably divine.

To cultivate SQ is to retrain attention itself—to learn not only to think or to feel but to listen with the soul. It is to live as if every silence conceals a syllable of revelation. The *Midbar* therefore is not a barren wasteland but a spiritual oasis. It's where Israel learned to listen, where the prophets learned to speak, and where each generation must return to reset its spiritual frequency.

THE WOMB OF THE WILDERNESS

In the Hebrew Bible, the number forty frequently symbolizes periods of transition and transformation. This number appears in several significant narratives: Noah's ark endures forty days and nights of flood, Moses spends forty days and nights on Mount Sinai receiving the Torah, Elijah retreats to the *Midbar* for forty days to escape King Ahab and Queen Jezebel, and the Israelites wander the *Midbar* for forty years en route to the promised land.

Now, what does this mystical forty symbolize? To grasp its significance, we look to the natural world, where one notable cycle of forty stands out—the forty-week gestational period of a human baby. Rabbinical sages also note that a fetus takes on the status of a potential life after forty days (Yevamot 69b). These biblical accounts of forty can be seen as a form of spiritual gestation. It's not a birth that follows but a rebirthing. A stage of life comes to an end just as a new one begins. Or, as the old saying goes, every new beginning grows out of another ending. Consider the Israelites: their forty-year journey reflects the passing of one generation, paving the way for a new one. The new generation becomes unburdened by the residual trauma of Egyptian slavery and the temptation of the golden calf. The wilderness serves as a womb for rebirth, nurturing a generation ready to enter the promised land with purity and transformation.

In Deuteronomy's closing chapters, the Israelites stand on the brink of the promised land, and Moses reflects on their forty-year wilderness journey:

> You have seen all that YHWH did before your very eyes in the land of Egypt, to Pharaoh and to all his servants and to his whole country: the wondrous feats that you saw with your own eyes, those great signs and marvels. Yet to this day YHWH has not given you a mind to understand, or eyes to see, or ears to hear. (Deut 29:1–3)

How is it that the Israelites, despite witnessing such marvels, have not fully perceived or understood them? The sage Rabba offers an insightful interpretation: a person may not truly grasp the wisdom imparted by a teacher until reaching forty years of age (Avot 5:21). This suggests that at forty, we experience a rebirth into what can be termed "middlescence"—a period in midlife characterized by self-discovery, reflection, and rebirth. It's a time akin to the *Midbar*, opening us to comprehend the wisdom we've accumulated and prepare for the next phase of life with deeper understanding.

It's noteworthy that I began to write this book at the age of forty during a sabbatical from my duties as a pulpit rabbi. This period away from the office, my personal *Midbar*, is a time for embracing a new chapter in my life and contributing something meaningful to the world. There are those who reach forty and carry out the cliche of the midlife crisis, seeing this time as a glass-half-empty waypoint in life, and thus try to experience as much novelty and excitement as they can. The *Midbar* isn't a place of crisis but of opportunity. Then again, the word for crisis in the Torah is משבר (*mashber*), which carries the additional meaning of being a birthing stool, reminding us that every crisis can give birth to blessing.[4] I see my own benchmark

4. A birthing stool is a piece of furniture designed to support women in a squatting or sitting position during childbirth. It typically features a U-shaped seat to provide comfort and facilitate the birthing process by using gravity to

of 40 as a midlife rebirthing stool, helping me transition into this period of life reflection and introspection. I personally have no desire for a new fancy sports car or motorcycle, or to go out thrill-seeking. But this is a time that I'm marking with a sense of rebirth, and like Hagar, encountering the questions "where have you come from, and where are you going?"

KENOSIS: EMPTYING SELF OF SELF

> Anyone who does not make themselves empty like the *Midbar* cannot acquire wisdom and the Torah
>
> —Bamidbar Rabbah 1:7

I first learned of the term "kenosis" from Scott Peck's book *Golf and the Spirit*. Golf and spirituality go hand-in-hand for me, yet I never thought one concept would simultaneously improve both my spiritual practice and my golf game until I learned what "kenosis" meant. Kenosis, as Peck describes it, is "the process of the self emptying itself of self, the point of being empty is not to have an empty mind; it is to make room for the new, the Other."[5] Of course, this idea forms an intriguing paradox—when we desire fullness, we first should seek emptiness. When I enter the tee box, my goal is to empty my mind of all the metrics associated with a successful swing. I set aside thoughts of tempo, club speed, tee height, my stance, and the importance of keeping my head down—elements that golfers typically obsess over with each swing. These are aspects I focus on at the driving range during practice sessions. However, when I'm actually on the course, I clear my mind and swing without the burden of accumulated golf wisdom. Scott Peck is right: this approach enhances not just my golf game but also my

---

assist in the birthing of the baby. This tool is often used to promote a more natural and upright position during labor, which can help in widening the pelvis and potentially reducing the duration of labor. Birthing stools have been used in various forms across different cultures and historical periods.

5. Peck, *Golf and the Spirit*, 40.

spiritual game too. This concept, though Christian in origin, has a spiritually universal application and has become an integral part of my personal Jewish practice. In Judaism, this idea is mirrored in the notion of becoming like the *Midbar*—a place devoid of worldly distractions, allowing the divine voice to be heard.

Put another way, we can understand kenosis as the metaphysical *Midbar*. This concept is vividly captured in a Hasidic story about Elimelech of Lizhensk, a revered rabbi from the 18th century. The tale describes how people would trail behind his carriage, a behavior that puzzles Elimelech. He asks his coachman why all the people are trailing behind, and the coachman explains that the people want to follow after wisdom and holiness. When Elimelech hears this, he decides that this is a good idea. He gets out and joins the people following the empty carriage. Although they might have sought to follow him initially, Elimelech's action teach a profound lesson: pursue not individuals but the essence of emptiness, for therein lies fulfillment. True wisdom emerges not merely from following mentors but through our capacity to become receptacles open to the insights of the universe. Venturing into the *Midbar* mirrors the chase after the empty carriage, a journey that teaches us emptiness diverges greatly from vanity. In the depths of profound emptiness, we discover the richest fullness.

A tale from the Talmud offers similar insights into the wisdom of kenosis. Rabbi Zeira, a sage from Babylonia, had been a master of the Babylonian Talmud, a compendium of legal commentary, Jewish lore, and biblical interpretations. A parallel Talmud was written concurrently in Israel on the same topics but with different understandings. Rabbi Zeira embarks on a regimen of a hundred fasts to deliberately shed all he had previously absorbed from the Babylonian Talmud (Bava Metzia 85a). Now, the question arises: why the need to relinquish his knowledge of the Babylonian Talmud to learn the Jerusalem Talmud? Rabbi Zeira's fasting isn't merely about emptying his stomach; it is an act of kenosis. He has to create a blank canvas within himself—a state of openness and receptivity that could accommodate the distinctive narrative and spirit of the Jerusalem Talmud.

Rabbi Zeira's act of "forgetting" wasn't about discarding knowledge but about making room for new understanding. It was his way of becoming like the *Midbar*, a metaphysical state of openness to embrace new Torah wisdom. By setting aside the preconceptions and familiarity of the Babylonian Talmud, he allowed new insights to root in his soul. This story highlights the essence of spiritual learning: the importance of emptying oneself to foster new growth. This concept has profound implications not just in religious study but in all aspects of life. Whether it's golf, Talmud, or personal development, making oneself empty like the wilderness is key to embracing change and growth. Rabbi Zeira's journey shows us that while we may naturally evolve due to life's experiences, intentional and conscious self-emptying is essential for profound personal transformation.

LIMINALITY—THE SPACE BETWEEN

Just days before my first child, Lilah, was born, I addressed my community on a Shabbat evening at Temple Beth Elohim, sharing my whirlwind of emotions about impending fatherhood. I spoke of my mingled fear and excitement, the blend of nervousness and joy. Questions raced through my mind: "What new responsibilities will I face?" "How will I balance my schedule?" and crucially, "Am I ready to be a father?" The term that encapsulated my emotional state was "liminal space," akin to being in the *Midbar*. Liminality implies being in transition, caught between two states. Derived from the Latin "limen," meaning "threshold," it captured my position: on the brink of fatherhood yet not quite there. Liminal moments between pregnancy and birth are where we imagine the possibilities of the future and dream of the blessings to come. It's where all of our old understandings of the world are becoming irrelevant, while the new ones are yet to take hold. When you're at the threshold, you're really in the *Midbar*.

Anthropologist Victor Turner notes that liminal moments are often likened to "death, to being in the womb, to invisibility, to darkness, to bisexuality, [and] to the wilderness."[6] We experience this amorphous inbetweeness of liminality most poignantly, he says, during cultural rites of passage such as bar mitzvahs, graduations, and weddings. If you ever reach a point in life where everything seems transitional, you might recognize it as being in a liminal space, or, in the language of our tradition, you are in the *Midbar*. For the Israelites, the *Midbar* represents an extended period of liminality, marking their transformative march from slavery in Egypt to freedom in the promised land. The *Midbar* serves not only as a womb, nurturing their growth and development but also as a threshold, a critical crossing point from their past to their future.

Liminal spaces are both scary and sacred. They are scary because they thrust us into the unknown, leaving us in an ambiguous state. Yet, they are sacred as they are often marked by rituals that foster a sense of holiness and create deep communal connections. Victor Turner dubs this transitional camaraderie as "communitas," the Latin word for community but also a term he employs to help us understand the intense fraternity we find in liminal rituals. When a child becomes a bar or bat mitzvah, the sacred transition not only permeates the adolescent who is taking their first steps into responsibility and adulthood but for the parents and family of the Bar or Bat Mitzvah, who become intertwined together in love, joy, and pride for the pivotal life cycle transition. For the Israelites, the liminality of the *Midbar* galvanizes the twelve tribes of Israel into a common communitas, a people forged in their transition between Egypt and the promised land.

The *Midbar* is a place of awe and sanctity where the Israelites experience the parting of the Sea of Reeds, receive the Torah at Mount Sinai, and build the tabernacle. However, it was also a place of uncertainty and fear, where the future seemed daunting and the longing for the past's predictability often surfaced. In your own liminal *Midbar*, it's natural to feel fear but also important to embrace the sacredness of these thresholds. They are the stepping stones to the destinations we are meant to reach. Lean into the

6. Turner, "Liminality and Communitas," 95–96.

holiness of these transitional moments, and take those steps forward into the future that awaits.

LIMINALITY ADDICTION

The child of the first person to enter the *Midbar*—Hagar—becomes the only figure in the Hebrew Bible to make the wilderness their permanent home. After Hagar returns to Abraham and Sarah, her circumstances deteriorate further once Ishmael is born. What began as an arrangement to fulfill God's promise of offspring unravels into jealousy and cruelty. Sarah's resentment grows, and Abraham, torn between his wives, sends Hagar and the boy away with only a skin of water and some bread.

Once again, Hagar finds herself in the *Midbar*, the same landscape where she had first fled in despair years earlier. The wilderness becomes the setting of her deepest anguish and her greatest revelation. When the water runs out, she places her child beneath a bush and steps away, unable to watch him die. Then, in that moment of emptiness, the divine voice breaks through again. As before, a divine messenger calls to her—but this time, the message changes. No longer is she told to return; now the Voice assures her of protection and promise, declaring that her son will live and become a great nation.

It is here, in the barrenness of the *Midbar*, that Ishmael's destiny takes root. "God was with the boy, and he grew, and he dwelt in the wilderness" (Gen 21:20). From that moment on, Ishmael never leaves. Others pass through the *Midbar*—Abraham, Moses, and the Israelites—but only Ishmael makes it his dwelling place. For him, the wilderness becomes not a passageway but a home. Yet while the *Midbar* can be a place of divine encounter and transformation, it is not meant to be a permanent address. The Israelites, after all, were called to move through it toward the promised land. Ishmael's dwelling there symbolizes what happens when liminality becomes a way of life—when transition itself becomes our identity.

While liminality can be holy, we're not meant to dwell in liminal spaces forever. Some people find themselves chasing liminality persistently, unable to settle, always looking for the next big change. They seem captivated by what might be ahead, often overlooking the blessings of their current situation. One such person was a congregant of mine, whose story is a telling example of this constant search for something new, while failing to realize the value of what he already had. Asher came to my office one day full of excitement about a significant change in his life. He planned to leave his successful career as a real estate broker to venture into the restaurant business. Despite the high failure rate of new restaurants, Asher dived into this venture with enthusiasm and initially found success.

However, after a few years, Asher grew restless and wanted to innovate further. He expanded his restaurant, adding new, refined dishes to the menu. But soon, even this wasn't enough. He started hosting pop-up restaurants within his own, constantly chasing new culinary trends and experiences.

This continuous pursuit of the next big thing eventually led to discontent with the restaurant industry itself. After a few more years, Asher closed his restaurant and moved on to another new venture. His pattern of constantly seeking something new, never fully content with his current success, seemed to be an ongoing cycle in his life. This behavior highlighted a common struggle: finding the balance between seeking new opportunities and appreciating what we already have. This phenomenon could be termed "liminality addiction," a state where the thrill of chasing the next opportunity overshadows the appreciation of the opportunity itself. To put it differently, it's as if one is ensnared by the allure of the *Midbar*, wandering endlessly in a threshold state, never acknowledging that to arrive at the promised land, all they must do is recognize the blessings of their current station and abandon the perpetual state of transition.

SOLITUDE AND SPIRITUAL REVELATION

Rabbi Nachman of Breslov, a Hasidic master and spiritual leader who lived from 1772 to 1810, was a great-grandson of the Baal

Shem Tov, the founder of Hasidic Judaism. Renowned for his profound spiritual insights and teachings, Rabbi Nachman's influence continues to resonate in the Jewish world and beyond. One of Rabbi Nachman's key teachings is the practice of *Hitbodedut*, or spiritual solitude. It's not about being lonely but about embracing the beauty of aloneness.

Hitbodedut is a form of unstructured, spontaneous prayer and meditation. It involves speaking to God in one's own words, as if conversing with a close friend, allowing the outpouring of innermost thoughts and feelings. Rabbi Nachman particularly recommended practicing *Hitbodedut* in nature, advocating for seclusion in the wilderness or forest to commune with one's thoughts and with God. He explained that in such settings, the natural world itself participates in and strengthens one's prayer:

> Know! when a person prays in the fields, all the flora enters into the prayer, helping him and strengthening his prayer. This is the reason prayer is called SiChah (conversation), the concept of "SiaCh (shrub) of the field" (Gen 2:5). All the shrubs of the field empower and assist his prayer.[7]

Hitbodedut was Rabbi Nachman's way of entering the *Midbar* and conversing with God. The act of withdrawing into nature to engage in this practice mirrors the journey of the Israelites in the *Midbar*, where they are able to escape overwhelming sounds of the cities of Egypt so that they could hear God's voice. One midrash accentuates this idea by picking up on an interesting superfluous word in the narrative of the exodus: "YHWH spoke to Moses and Aaron in the land of Egypt" (Exod 12:1). Why does it bother saying "in the land of Egypt"? Where else would they be? The Israelites haven't been anywhere else for over four hundred years! The midrash therefore highlights that the words "in the land of Egypt" refer specifically to the space outside the cities of Egypt (Mekhilta d'Rabbi Ishmael, Pisḥa 1:8). Just as it's impossible to have a conversation in a noisy bar, the cities are far too polluted with commotion

7. Likutei Moharan, Part II 11:1:1

and distractions for us to hear the murmuring voice of God. To do so, we need to immerse ourselves in *Midbar*.

Of course, other faith traditions pick up on this idea as well. Rumi, the Sufi mystic and poet whose poem was referenced in the previous chapter, writes a poem that sounds like it could have been written by Rabbi Nachman. In his work entitled "A Great Wagon," Rumi writes:

> Beyond all notions of right and wrong,
> there opens a vast meadow.
> I will meet you there—
> where the soul rests upon the soft earth,
> and the world becomes too full for words.
> In that stillness, even "you" and "I"
> no longer make sense.[8]

Cultural individualism bears a negative connotation, but this kind of spiritual individualism, the variety where "each other" gives way to self-encounter, harbors a life-changing beauty. Both Rumi and Rabbi Nachman highlight that genuine understanding and connection, especially in nature's solitude, surpass our usual modes of communication and societal norms. They suggest that profound insights lie within us, best accessed in solitude.

Rabbi Nachman's teachings on *Hitbodedut* not only encourage personal spiritual growth but also echo a broader theme found throughout Jewish history: the use of *Midbar* as a means to achieve deeper self-understanding and a closer relationship with the Divine. To be in the metaphysical state of *Midbar*, one need not necessarily traverse the wilderness. However, the physical space within nature incubates the experience of *Midbar*. For me, I go for hikes in the woods alone; I sit on the bluffs overlooking the Long Island Sound and listen to the brilliant harmonies of nature; I sometimes go camping by myself to a place with no cellphone service and minimal amenities, so that I can connect more deeply with myself and with God. Where do you find your *Midbar*, your place of solitude and spiritual revelation?

8. Jalāl al-Dīn Rūmī, *Dīvān-e Shams-e Tabrīzī*, rubāʿī 157. English translation by the author from the original Persian (public domain).

QUESTIONS FOR CONSIDERATION:

1. **Understanding *Midbar* in Personal Contexts:** How can the concept of *Midbar* be applied in our personal lives to enhance self-awareness and spiritual growth?
2. **Solitude's Role in Modern Life:** In an age dominated by technology and constant connectivity, what role does solitude play in maintaining mental and spiritual well-being?
3. **The Intersection of Solitude and Community in Spiritual Practice:** How do solitary practices like *Hitbodedut* complement communal religious practices in fostering a holistic spiritual life?
4. **Defining Liminal Spaces:** How would you define a liminal space in your own words, and what are some examples of liminal spaces in everyday life? Can you recall a time in your life when you felt you were in a liminal space, transitioning from one phase to another? What was this experience like?
5. **Kenosis and Modern Challenges:** How might the concept of Kenosis be relevant or beneficial in addressing contemporary life challenges, such as stress, materialism, or loss of community?

5

Mara

Embrace Bitterness and Let It Be Your Teacher

שֶׁבְּכָל הַלֵּילוֹת אָנוּ אוֹכְלִין שְׁאָר יְרָקוֹת, הַלַּיְלָה הַזֶּה מָרוֹר

Why on all other nights do we eat all sorts of herbs but on this night, ones that are particularly bitter (*maror*)?

—Passover Haggadah

The Jewish rituals of Passover require that Jews not only ask questions at a Seder (a ritualized meal) regarding the bitterness of slavery but that we taste the bitterness ourselves. The tradition is for Jews to eat a bitter herb known as *maror*, which often takes the form of horseradish in Ashkenazic Jewish households and a bitter lettuce in Sephardic homes. The tableau of eating bitterness is generally regarded as enabling us to taste the bitterness of slavery and of Egypt. Most Jews who partake in this ritual eat a grated horseradish, often mixed with vinegar and beet juice, which slightly tempers its harshness. A bit of sweet paste called *charoset*, made from ground apples, nuts, and wine, can be combined with the maror to further temper its harshness. Personally, I find the biggest piece of raw horseradish sliced directly from the root and lean hard into the taste of bitterness, knowing that maror not only reminds us of slavery but also teaches us what it means to be free. Many Sephardic and Mizrachi Jews underscore the significance of consuming the bitter herb during Passover by placing it prominently at the center of the Seder plate, elevated above the other symbolic elements: the egg (representing life), charoset (denoting sweetness and the mortar used by the Israelites in Egypt), a lamb bone (symbolizing the ancient Passover sacrifice), and a green vegetable (signifying springtime). As much as the Jewish tradition reminds us to allow the bitterness to be a vehicle to experience Egypt, the bitter herb more profoundly transports us to a different metaphysical landscape: a place called Mara.

WHERE IS MARA?

As the Israelites embark on their exodus from Egypt, their journey unfolds over forty years through a series of stops within the wilderness. Some of these locations are tangible on maps, while others, like Eden, exist more as profound waypoints in the human experience. The metaphysical wanderings chart a course of spiritual locations that we can see reflected throughout the Hebrew Bible and within our own lives. Among these pivotal stops is Mara. Following the awe-inspiring miracle at the Sea of Reeds, the Israelites journey three days before arriving at this location. During that time, the wonder of the waters parted begins to fade as they are unable to find water.

> "They came to Mara, but they could not drink the water from Mara, for it was bitter (*marim*). Therefore, it was named Mara." (Exod 15:23)

The exact geography of Mara remains elusive, yet more significant than its locale is Mara's metaphysical essence, a universal experience of embracing bitterness and struggle that imparts profound lessons. The name "Mara," derived from the bitterness of its waters, *marim* (מרים), offers more than a mere description; it opens a portal to deeper understanding. The linguistic interplay in the name Mara invites endless etymological explorations by commentators. The word *marim* מָרִים, while describing bitterness, also echoes several heteronyms including *morim* מֹרִים (rebels) and Miriam מִרְיָם, Moses' sister, who according to Jewish legend, provides a traveling well to sustain the Israelites in the wilderness. It's perhaps not a coincidence that a heteronym of *mar*, spelled מָר (bitterness), is the word מֹר (myrrh), the ancient biblical perfume that was used as incense in the Jerusalem Temple, as well as a core ingredient in the oil used to anoint the kings of Judah. Additionally, *marim* resonates with the Hebrew word for teacher, *morah* מוֹרָה, suggesting that life's bitter waters can also be profound instructors.

When Moses pleads for assistance, God reveals to him a tree to be cast (יורהו *yorehu*) into the bitter waters to sweeten them. The root י-ר-ה, evident in "יורהו *yorehu*," conveys several meanings: to show, to shoot, and—most critically—to teach. This word foreshadows not only the lessons derived from bitterness but also the Torah תורה (teaching) itself, which shares the same etymology. The essential laws and wisdom that the Israelites are soon to receive at Sinai emerge from the bitterness experienced in Egypt. This raises the question: What type of tree could alleviate bitterness? Drawing from Proverbs in the Bible, commentators suggest, "It (Torah) is a tree of life to those who embrace it, and its supporters find happiness" (Prov 3:18).[1] Avoiding bitterness doesn't reduce its impact on us; instead, we should embrace it, recognizing that adversity can be our most significant teacher. This view advocates for reinterpreting life's bitter moments not as ultimate setbacks but as opportunities to find hidden sweetness and wisdom.

THE MARA-THON

As I hit mile 20 of a 26.2-mile marathon, my body starts to revolt—legs heavy, lungs burning, mind begging me to stop. That's

1. See Tzror HaMor on Exod 15:23. This commentary on the Torah was composed by Abraham Saba (1460–510 CE) and contains interpretations according to both the plain sense as well as the mystical teachings of the Zohar.

when I turn to mantras, whispered first in my head and then aloud, like lifelines I can hold onto. The one I return to most comes from an obscure rabbi mentioned only once in all of rabbinic literature. Ben Hai Hai teaches, "לְפוּם צַעֲרָא אַגְרָא—according to the suffering is the reward" (Avot 5:26). Not reward as compensation but reward as transformation. Growth comes where comfort ends.

People often ask me why I love running marathons. The honest answer is: I don't. I hate running. I hate leaving my bed before sunrise, stepping into the cold, and forcing my legs to move when they would much rather be still. Blisters form, toenails disappear, muscles ache in places I didn't know existed. I don't run because I enjoy the experience—I run because I value what the experience builds within me.

Running, then, is a kind of Mara-thon—a chosen bitterness. Every mile is mildly unpleasant. Some are excruciating. A marathon demands presence, discipline, patience, and an ability to keep going when everything inside you would rather stop. It is Mara in manageable doses, bitterness we intentionally enter so that we can learn from it.

Cyclists express this openly. Fausto Coppi famously said, "Cycling is suffering." Eddy Merckx added, "Cyclists live with pain. If you can't handle it, you will win nothing." Olympian Scott Martin described cycling as being "a student of pain."[2] Watch the Tour de France and when you see the cyclists reach a mountain, simply watch their faces—every grimace, every labored breath tells the story of Mara. Success isn't built by escaping discomfort but by learning to move through it.

This is the essence of "according to the suffering is the reward (Avot 5:26). Not glorifying pain or seeking suffering for its own sake. Rather, recognizing that resilience, empathy, and inner strength are often learned in the places we would never choose willingly—and sometimes in the places we choose precisely to practice enduring them. Running trains me for the Mara I do not choose. It reminds me that pain is survivable, that discomfort is temporary, and that continuing forward—even slowly—is an

2. Daly, "Taking the Pain."

opportunity for growth and character development. A Mara-thon gives me rehearsal space for the grief, loss, and uncertainty that life thrusts upon us.

Some suffering in life runs toward us. Some we run toward. Both have something to teach, if we are willing to listen. A marathon is long. Mara is bitter. But step by step—mile by mile—bitterness becomes a teacher.

CALL ME MARA (BITTERNESS)

In the biblical book of Ruth, we discover the bereaved matriarch Naomi, who navigates through the bitter waters of loss: the passing of her husband, Elimelech, and her sons, Mahlon and Chilion. This family, originally rooted in Bethlehem of Judea, had journeyed to Moab. Here, Naomi's sons wed Moabite women, Ruth and Orpah. Upon the tragic demise of her husband and sons, Naomi, enveloped in sorrow, decides to return to Judah. She urges her daughters-in-law to remain in Moab, their homeland, foreseeing a brighter future for them there. Naomi expresses her anguish: "My lot is greatly more bitter (*mar*) than yours" (Ruth 1:13). Amidst tears and heartache, Orpah heeds Naomi's counsel, but Ruth, with steadfast loyalty, declares, "Wherever you go, I will go, wherever you lodge, I will lodge, your people shall be my people, and your God my God" (Ruth 1:17). Ruth attaches herself to Naomi, and the two head to Bethlehem together.

Upon their arrival in Bethlehem, the townspeople who are excited to see them inquire, "Can this be Naomi?" At this point, Naomi does something strange: she personifies her bitterness and says, "Do not call me Naomi," a name whose etymology refers to pleasantness and sweetness. Instead, she insists, "Call me Mara (bitterness), for Shaddai (God) has made my lot exceedingly bitter" (Ruth 1:20). Naomi perceives her return as a journey from fullness to emptiness. Can Naomi truly be so oblivious to the blessing she possesses in Ruth, whose devotion transcends cultural and geographical boundaries? How can Naomi claim emptiness when accompanied by such unwavering love? Intriguingly, the narrative ceases to refer to Naomi as Mara. This omission beckons us to inquire, "Where is Naomi?"—not in a physical sense but in her metaphysical state. The story does not echo her chosen name of Mara; instead, it reveals her immersion in the state of Mara, a place where the hidden teachings of bitterness are yet to be unveiled.

The story culminates with Ruth's marriage to Boaz, Naomi's kinsman, and the birth of a child that brings joy and renewal to Naomi's life. The community exclaims, "A child is born to Naomi!" From the depths of her bitterness and perceived emptiness, Naomi evolves, recognizing that life can transform into a rich and flavorful existence. What appears empty may indeed be laden with unseen blessings.

This narrative invites us to reflect on our own encounters with bitterness. In our journeys through the metaphysical Mara, the challenge lies not in becoming embittered but in discerning the lessons bitterness imparts. It is in these moments of profound sorrow that we are offered an opportunity to not only comprehend our trials but to discover the hidden blessings that have always been present yet perhaps unnoticed. Naomi's journey from bitterness to renewal reminds us that in every experience of Mara, there is a potential for profound transformation and enlightenment.

MARA AND LOGOTHEORY

In this poignant narrative, Naomi's transformation from bitterness to renewal embodies Viktor Frankl's understanding of deriving meaning from trauma. Frankl, a Holocaust survivor and psychiatrist, believed that even in the most bitter and dehumanizing experiences, individuals could find meaning and purpose. Naomi's story, set against the backdrop of Mara, embodies what Frankl discovered through his own experiences at Auschwitz.

Frankl, in his international best-seller *Man's Search for Meaning*, argues that our response to suffering is what defines us, not the suffering itself. Frankl reflected that at one point during his imprisonment in Auschwitz, he thought:

> It seemed to me that I would die in the near future. In this critical situation, however, my concern was different from that of most of my comrades. Their question was, "Will we survive the camp? For, if not, all this suffering has no meaning." The question which beset me was, "Has all this suffering, this dying around us, a meaning? For, if not, then ultimately there is no meaning to survival; for a life whose meaning depends upon such a happenstance—as whether one escapes or not ultimately would not be worth living at all."[3]

Frankl relates that in every moment of unimaginable suffering, there is an opportunity for growth and learning. We find this paradigm reflected through Naomi's journey as well. Initially, she is consumed by her bitterness, feeling that life has left her with nothing but pain. However, as the story progresses, Naomi develops a new understanding of her bitterness. She opens her eyes to what was right before her, but she neglected to see the love and loyalty of Ruth. This shift in perspective provided countless Auschwitz prisoners with the tools they needed to prevent falling into despair.

According to Frankl, the search for meaning embodies the primary motivation in human life. Those who lose it lose themselves and are often consumed by their trauma. This meaning can be found in various forms: in work, in love, and in courage during difficult times. Naomi's eventual recognition of the blessings in her life, even amidst her suffering, reflects the concept that meaning can often be found in the most bitter of experiences. Her ability to embrace the love and support of Ruth, and later the joy of Boaz and their child, shows a movement from mere survival in her trauma, to finding a deeper significance and joy in life.

Frankl's theory, known as logotherapy, suggests that by finding meaning in suffering, one can endure it with a sense of purpose. Naomi's journey from Mara, a symbol of bitterness, to a place of gratitude and renewal, illustrates this concept. It demonstrates that our most challenging experiences can lead to profound personal growth and fulfillment. This story, much like

3. Frankl, *Man's Search for Meaning*, 115.

the Israelites' experience in Mara, highlights the human capacity to find meaning in life's bitter waters, transforming them into a source of strength and wisdom. Frankl's teachings echo the experience of Mara in that they remind us to see our trials not as mere afflictions but as life's greatest teachers. Even in our deepest sorrows, there lies the potential for discovering profound meaning and experiencing significant growth.

THE QUESTION ISN'T "WHY DO WE EXPERIENCE BITTERNESS?"

One of the most misquoted Jewish book titles of all time happens to also be one of the best-selling contemporary non-fiction Jewish books of all-time. Following the death of his son, Rabbi Harold Kushner published the book *When Bad Things Happen to Good People*. People who reference the book often cite it as *Why Bad Things Happen to Good People* because they are captivated by the timeless question of theodicy, that is, they seek to explain the very nature of why we suffer. Kushner's actual title suggests a different way to look at the world, that is, bad things will inevitably happen to good people, to bad people, and to each and every one of us. The question is not why bad things happen but rather, how we respond in life to when they do happen.[4]

The biblical mindset was predominantly focused on sin being the catalyst for our suffering. Moses teaches the Israelites in the book of Leviticus:

> But if you do not listen to me, and do not observe all these commandments . . . .
>
> Then I will set my face against you, you will be hit by plague in the face of your enemies; those who hate you will route you, you will flee, with no one pursuing you. (Lev 26:14, 17)

Through this perspective, suffering relates to our misbehavior or lack of following the laws that God set out for us. Of course, even

4. Kushner, *When Bad Things Happen*.

many biblical minds struggled with this worldview when they saw wicked people prosper and rationalized this by noting that eventually, evil would have its day of judgment. In this vein, the psalmist writes:

> A brutish man cannot know, a fool cannot understand this: though the wicked sprout like grass, though all evildoers blossom, it is only that they may be destroyed forever. (Ps 92:7–8)

In other words, it may seem that the wicked are successful, but the more they flourish, the harder their eventual crash will be. Even this perspective falls short of the reality people witness in their lives. The righteous often suffer bitterness just as much as those who are ignoble, giving way to the biblical Job, who witnesses that "[the wicked] spend their days in happiness, and go down to the grave in peace (Job 21:13)." A wholly righteous man, Job seemingly had it all until God decides to take everything away from him for no fault of his own. Job loses his wealth, his health, and most of his family, none of which was caused by Job's sins or lack of upright behavior. After exploring theological causes for suffering, and after chapters of crying out to God for answers, Job finally receives the message that the way of the world is beyond human understanding. Job's experience most closely echoes the reality through which Kushner experiences the world in the wake of the tragic loss of his son Aaron.

Seeing suffering as a result of God's punishment isn't just philosophically hard to rationalize—it poisons our self-image. As Kushner emphasizes, "It teaches people to blame themselves. It creates guilt even where there is no basis for guilt. It makes people hate God, even as it makes them hate themselves. And most disturbing of all, it does not even fit the facts."[5] Bad things happen to each and every one us regardless of our behavior, the question is not why, but now that it has happened, how can we learn about ourselves and grow from the experience? Or, put another way, how do we turn our bitterness into Torah, our suffering into meaning?

5. Kushner, *When Bad Things Happen*, 10.

And if we get hung up on the cause of our suffering, we might simply follow the example of Job and surrender to trusting in God as we accept that some things in this world are simply beyond our comprehension.

IN GRIEF, WE LEARN TO SWEETEN THE BITTERNESS OF OTHERS

The Psalmist said that in his affliction, he learned the law of God.
And in truth, grief is a great teacher, when it sends us back to serve
and bless the living. We learn how to counsel and comfort those who,
like ourselves, are bowed with sorrow. We learn to keep silent in their
presences, and when a word will assure them of our love and concern.
Thus, even when they are gone, the departed are with us, moving us
to live as, in their higher moments, they themselves wished to live.
We remember them now; they live in our hearts; they are a blessing

—Rabbi Chaim Stern[6]

When I join families in their grief during shiva, I often share this liturgical piece. Shiva, the seven-day mourning period following the burial in Jewish tradition, involves families receiving comfort from visitors who provide food and companionship. During these times of sorrow, people often resort to clichéd consolations like "they're in a better place now," "God doesn't give you more than you can handle," or "everything happens for a reason." Such platitudes, while well-intentioned, can be more hurtful than helpful. We too often feel the need to try to say the right thing, even when we don't have the right thing to say. Bitterness cannot be sweetened with trite words that we don't even ourselves believe. And even when we have impactful words to offer, mourners may not be ready to hear them. Rabbi Chaim Stern's words are not a one-size-fits-all expression of what to say to the mourner. But used

6. Stern, *Gates of Prayer*, 593. Reprinted with permission from the CCAR Press.

correctly, they offer those in one of the most bitter periods in their lives an avenue to lean into their bitterness and use it as a tool for growth and blessing.

Rabbi Shimon Ben Gamliel, reflecting on how God sweetens the bitter waters of Mara, notes that God uses an olive tree, known for its bitterness, for this purpose. He interprets this as God healing bitterness with bitterness (מרפא את המר במר). The remedy for grief isn't always found in its opposite but rather in understanding and embracing the nature of our sorrow. It's about acknowledging our emotions, not masking them with hollow words (Mekhilta D'Rabbi Yishmael, Vayassa 1:17).

When my family buried my mother-in-law, Carol, after a year-long struggle with lung cancer, we all partook in the Jewish tradition of shoveling earth on her casket. The tradition requires mourners to at least cover the casket with a layer of earth before reciting a prayer of mourning known as the Kaddish. Typically, the cemetery workers fill in the rest of the grave after the family leaves, but I decided to stay behind to finish the job myself. I wasn't even halfway done when my hands started to swell. A blood blister on my right palm below the ring on my left ring-finger turned a deep crimson. The sides of both hands had by now throbbed with cuts. I hadn't brought gloves, and the old and well-used wooden handle of the shovel wasn't kind to my hands, it felt like sandpaper against my skin. I clenched my teeth and grimaced through shovel after shovel in what seemed like an endless task. I was in no rush, though, to the chagrin of the cemetery manager who scowled at me as if my mourning was an inconvenience to him. Perhaps his insurance company required him to supervise. In some ways, I felt this was the last act of love that I could offer to Carol, but it was mostly about confronting the bitter pill of loss, feeling in my hands the way that my heart felt on the inside, and facing the reality that my mother-in-law Carol was truly gone. Yes, filling in her grave was painful both physically and emotionally, but it was also cathartic. It was healing my spiritual bitterness with physical bitterness. My hands and my back ached, but my heart somehow felt a bit lighter and slightly mended.

Jewish mourning rituals encourage mourners to actively engage with their grief rather than conceal it in their subconscious. Through a practice known as kriyah (tearing), individuals tear their clothes as a visceral representation of their inner turmoil and devastation. They wear their brokenness not only for the world to see but to be reminded themselves that one of the first steps to healing is embracing the feeling of bitterness. Beyond the period of mourning, when the torn clothes are put aside, Jews often keep the wounds of grief open through telling stories of their loved ones, by continuing to recite Mourner's Kaddish and by embracing the bitterness one painful act at a time. No, we don't move on from our grief; rather, we just learn to move with it. The Jewish way is not the fun or easy way but is rooted in the belief that it's a healthy way to process an ongoing painful void that loss leaves in our lives. Bitterness is not only a great teacher but a great healer.

The process of healing from grief involves a challenging journey through the layers of our sorrow. It's about finding meaning and growth in our suffering, much like the olive treem, which, despite its initial bitterness, eventually yields fruit and oil that are cherished for their richness and depth. In the moments of our deepest grief, we are offered an opportunity to grow, to develop a deeper compassion for ourselves and others, and to connect more profoundly with the complexities of human emotion. Rabbi Stern's words and Rabbi Shimon Ben Gamliel's interpretation together weave a narrative that invites us to view grief not just as a bitter experience to be sweetened but as a profound teacher that shapes us into more empathetic and understanding beings.

WELCOMING MARA AS A GUEST

This body is a guesthouse, my friend.
Each morning, someone new comes running in—
a joy, a sorrow, a sudden meanness,
some fleeting awareness knocking at your door.
Welcome them all, and give them a seat.

Don't say, "This one will linger, a weight upon my neck,"
for soon enough it will vanish into nothingness.
Whatever arrives from the unseen world,
receive it in your heart—treat it kindly, as an honored guest.

—RUMI[7]

Rumi, born Jalāl ad-Dīn Muhammad Rūmī in 1207 in present-day Afghanistan, was a 13th-century Persian poet, Islamic scholar, theologian, and Sufi mystic. In his poem "Guest House," Rumi offers us the image of treating emotions as guests at our house, a place in which all are welcome. "Welcome them all!" exclaims Rumi, even the ones that we would typically be inclined to keep out. To this end, moments of bitterness and hardship aren't unwelcome visitors; when we welcome them, they become "emotions that guide us."

Rumi, although writing as a Muslim mystic, inspires a universal message about emotions in his poem, one in alignment with how we can understand the Israelite experience at Mara and Naomi's experience of becoming Mara. Despite its unappetizing taste, we welcome bitterness as a core ingredient to the palate of spiritual living. Our inclination might be to hide from it, to mask it, or even feel shame for feeling it, but when we embrace it, we unlock the deep wisdom hidden under its facade.

The Pixar animated film *Inside Out* offers us an anthropomorphized version of Rumi's teachings. In *Inside Out*, emotions are personified and given center-stage, showing the inner workings of a young girl named Riley's mind as she navigates through

7. Adapted from the Persian original of Jalal al-Din Rumi, "The Guest House," from *Masnavi-i Ma'navi* (Book II, lines 1129–1134):

هست مهمانخانه این تن ای جوان
هر صباحی ضیف نو آید دوان
هین مگو کین ماند اندر گردنم
که همکنون بازپرد در عدم
هرچه آید از جهان غیب پوش
در دلت ضیف است او را دار خوش

Translation rendered from the public domain Persian text, inspired by earlier English versions including those of Coleman Barks and Kabir Helminski.

a significant life change. Joy, Sadness, Anger, Fear, and Disgust are each characters that play a pivotal role in shaping her experiences and reactions. The movie begins by Joy dominating the life of this budding child. Joy is able to find value and a role for certain negative emotions like Anger, Fear, and Disgust but cannot comprehend the positive role of sadness in life. Joy therefore tries to relegate sadness to a confined circle. Drawing a chalk circle on the floor little bigger than a single step wide, Joy tells Sadness, "This is the circle of sadness; your job is to stay inside of it." Of course, Joy comes to learn the obvious: we cannot confine any of our emotions, nor can we bottle them up. Only toward the end of the film does Joy come to realize that all emotions, including Sadness, have their unique and essential role in Riley's life. As the story progresses, Joy's understanding evolves: she comes to understand Sadness as an integral part of being human.[8] This realization is beautifully aligned with Rumi's message in "The Guest House," where every emotion is a guest, bringing its own gift. The film powerfully illustrates this concept when Sadness helps Riley to express her true feelings to her parents, leading to a cathartic moment of bonding and understanding. This pivotal scene teaches that embracing and expressing all our emotions, even those that are uncomfortable, everything from sadness to bitterness, is crucial for genuine connection and growth.

In essence, *Inside Out*, much like Rumi's poem, teaches us that the richness of our emotional landscape, with its diverse range of feelings, is what makes us fully human. It underscores the idea that emotional health and maturity come not from suppressing or controlling our emotions but from welcoming and understanding them as vital parts of our inner selves, each contributing to our overall well-being and each offering us a profound teaching about life and our lives.

We can find similar universal wisdom to Rumi's in the legends of Buddhism. In Buddhism, the powerful demon god who challenges the Buddha is coincidentally named Mara. This name in Sanskrit is not derived from bitterness but rather from death.

8. Docter, *Inside Out*.

Over time, Mara has become a symbol for various negative emotions, including lust, greed, anger, doubt, and bitterness. According to a story shared by Buddhist psychologist Tara Brach, the Buddha would not turn Mara away but instead invite him for tea. The Buddha would calmly acknowledge Mara's presence with the words "I see you, Mara!"[9]

Echoing Rumi, our challenge becomes to invite Mara, our bitterness, to a cup of tea. Sit with it, talk with it, entertain it, even let it linger for a bit but most importantly, learn from it. If you have welcomed Mara into your home, or if you find yourself in the metaphysical space of Mara, learn into appreciate it, and most importantly, let it be your teacher.

WHAT TO DO WITH ALL THIS BITTERNESS

The journey through Mara teaches an essential lesson about the human condition. The Israelites' passage through the wilderness and Naomi's transformation from bitterness to renewal, mirrored in the stories of *Inside Out* and the teachings of Rumi and Buddhism, all converge on a singular truth: the embrace of every emotion and experience is a vital part of our existence. This chapter, delving into the depths of human sorrow and pain, illustrates that life's bitterness, much like the bitter waters of Mara, is not a curse to be shunned but a catalyst for profound growth and enlightenment. It is in the acceptance and understanding of our own Mara moments, our own encounters with grief, loss, and hardship, that we find the keys to deeper wisdom and a more fulfilling life. By welcoming each emotion, each challenge as a guest, we open ourselves to a more complete and compassionate understanding of our journey, transforming our bitterest experiences into the sweetest lessons. This perspective does not diminish the pain or struggle but empowers us to find meaning and purpose within it, much like Naomi finding joy in the life she thought was bitter and Riley learning the value of all her emotions. As we traverse

9. Brach, *Radical Acceptance*, 75–76.

our own wilderness, we should consider embracing the lesson of Mara—that is, moments of *mar* (bitterness) often go in tandem the sweetness of the tree of life (Torah). And when you open your eyes and discover the tree of life, you may be closer than you ever imagined to glimpsing Eden. Mara offers us a window to discover the profound sweetness hidden within life's inevitable suffering.

QUESTIONS FOR CONSIDERATION

1. **The Metaphysical Significance of Mara:** How does the metaphysical interpretation of Mara as a place of bitterness and learning challenge or reinforce your understanding of hardships in your own life?
2. **Naomi's Transformation:** In what ways can Naomi's journey from bitterness to renewal in the book of Ruth be seen as a reflection of our own processes of dealing with grief and loss? Are there personal experiences in your life that parallel her journey?
3. **Viktor Frankl's Logotherapy:** Considering Frankl's idea that finding meaning in suffering can transform our perspective, how can we apply this principle to our own moments of struggle and despair?
4. **Lessons from Grief and Compassion:** Drawing from the chapter's exploration of grief and Rabbi Chaim Stern's teachings, how can personal experiences of sorrow and bitterness enhance our ability to empathize with and support others in their times of hardship?
5. **Rumi's "Guest House" and Embracing Emotions:** How does Rumi's concept of treating each emotion as a guest change your approach to dealing with negative feelings or experiences? Can you recall a situation where welcoming and learning from a "negative" emotion led to personal growth?

6

Mitzrayim

The Narrow Space

חַיָּב אָדָם לִרְאוֹת אֶת עַצְמוֹ כְּאִלּוּ הוּא יָצָא מִמִּצְרַיִם,

Each person is required to see themselves as if they left Egypt

—Passover Haggadah

Every year, as I read this line from the Passover Haggadah, I try to immerse myself in the array of experiences and emotions that spanned the era of enslavement in Egypt to the exodus of the Hebrews from Egypt. It's an attempt to transport my consciousness into the memory of a time and a place beyond my own experiences, a place known as Egypt, or *Mitzrayim* in Hebrew. Such an act might defy how we typically understand human memory and consciousness, but in the spiritual world, we have a name for this kind of memory. The Greek Philosopher Plato coined the term "anamnesis" to describe the way the human soul is imprinted with recollections of things that happened long before we were born but which we uncover through a spiritual practice. Christianity adopted this term to refer to the living memory that connects the faithful with the foundational events of the Christian faith. Jews similarly use the word "*zecher* זכר" to describe this spiritual remembrance of the past. To see ourselves as if we left Egypt isn't about physically going to Egypt; it's about tapping into this metaphysical place that can play out in any time and any place.

The Hebrew name *Mitzrayim* may be translated simply as "Egypt," yet the name *Mitzrayim* carries with it metaphysical undertones that transcend its geographical borders, encompassing both a physical place and a spiritual realm rich with layers. In the literal sense, *Mitzrayim* is the land of the Nile, a place where the biblical patriarchs and matriarchs sought refuge during times of famine. It is the very place where the modern country of Egypt, still referred to as *Mitzrayim* by Israelis, exists today. It is a land of paradoxes, where Joseph rose from slavery to become a powerful ruler, where Moses was born in the shadow of oppression, and where the Israelites endured centuries of servitude. It represents both the suffocating stranglehold of bondage and the hope of liberation.

There are two possible etymological roots for *Mitzrayim* (מִצְרַיִם): the first is that it stems from מ-צ-ר, meaning to border, to shut, or to limit. The other, equally as plausible, is that it comes from just the two letters צ-ר, which means narrowness, distress, to be restricted, or to be tied up. "*Meitzar*" refers to a constricted space, with its plural form being "*Mitzrayim*." Egypt in the ancient world was broken up into Lower and Upper Egypt, each of which was its own *meitzar*, and collectively formed *Mitzrayim*. To be in *Mitzrayim* is to be within the narrow straits, to be in a state of constriction, strangled by our own fears, doubts, and insecurities. Just as the Israelites yearned for freedom from the bondage of Pharaoh, in every day and age, we find ourselves as individuals and communities who yearn to break free from the chains that bind us.

The exodus from *Mitzrayim*, therefore, holds a universal message. It is a journey from narrowness to the expanse, from angst to relief, and from bondage to liberation; it symbolizes the human capacity to break the yokes that bind us, and liberate ourselves from constriction. *Mitzrayim* teaches us that true freedom is not only physical but also spiritual and emotional.

In every generation, it is a fundamental requirement for each individual to envision themselves as if they personally left *Mitzrayim* (Egypt). While one need not physically journey to Egypt to fulfill the directive of the Passover Haggadah, the essence of *Mitzrayim* is a profound aspect of our consciousness, one that invites exploration throughout our lives. The justification for this commandment that the rabbis offer cites a biblical text from Exodus: "And you are to tell your child on that day, saying: It is because of what YHWH did for *me*, when I went out of Egypt" (Exod 13:8). The emphasis of this proof text is the word "me." Your role isn't to connect your fate to our ancestors but to connect *Mitzrayim* to your personal narrative. The sage Rava echoes this point when elucidating the requirement: "When mentioning the exodus from Egypt," he writes, "one must emphasize: And God took *us* out from there" (Pesachim 116b). In this way, a primary responsibility of participants at a Passover Seder is to recognize the way that God loosened the constraints that bound *you*.

FROM NARROWNESS TO THE EXPANSE

אֵלֶּה מַסְעֵי בְנֵי־יִשְׂרָאֵל אֲשֶׁר יָצְאוּ מֵאֶרֶץ מִצְרַיִם

These are the journeys of the Children of Israel when
they went forth from the land of Egypt

—Num 33:1

The book of Numbers records forty-two stops or journeys of the Israelites in their wanderings from Egypt to the promised land. Rabbi Menachem Mendell Schneerson, also known as the Lubavitcher Rebbe, points out that if we read the text literally, only the first of the recorded journeys—from Rameses to Succot—constituted a "going forth from the land of Egypt." The other forty-one journeys described were all made outside the land of Egypt, within the *Midbar*. We can see this either as a geographic contradiction or look beyond map. Schneerson teaches that "for every journey that brought them nearer to the land of Israel and their destiny made the previous stopping point seem like a confinement, another Egypt. Each stage was a new exodus. They had already left the physical Egypt. But they still had to pass beyond the Egypt, the narrowness of the soul."[1]

Even as the Israelites roamed through the expansive wilderness of the *Midbar*, their souls remain imprisoned in spiritual confinement. Their persistent complaints, exemplified by statements like "if only we had meat to eat! We remember the fish we ate in Egypt at no cost—also the cucumbers, melons, leeks, onions, and garlic" (Num 11:4–5), showcase their reluctance to free themselves from the mental bonds of Egypt, despite having physically departed from its borders. This mindset ultimately leads them down the perilous path of idolatry, as they construct and exalt a golden calf—an idol that resonated with the worship of the Egyptian bull god Apis.

Throughout their wanderings, it becomes evident that even though they have physically left the land of Egypt, their spirits remain confined within the emotional and spiritual limitations of *Mitzrayim*. In essence, this underscores that while you can indeed remove the Israelites from *Mitzrayim*, extracting *Mitzrayim* from the depths of the Israelite psyche proves more challenging.

TZARAAT: THE SPIRITUAL AFFLICTION OF DWELLING IN *MITZRAYIM* WHILE PHYSICALLY FREE

In the Hebrew Bible, there is mention of a contagious ailment afflicting the Israelites during their wanderings, referred to as "*tzaraat*." While the King James Bible interprets it as leprosy, most scholars believe it is something different, something not entirely understood. *Tzaraat* presents various symptoms, including skin rashes, discoloration, baldness, and white scales. Modern medical scholars identify the white spots described in *tzaraat* as vitiligo, a disfiguring yet benign condition, or as psoriasis, which results in silvery scales and itchy, red patches on the skin. *Tzaraat*, though

1. Likkutei Sichot, Vol. II, 348–53

often translated as "leprosy," bears little resemblance to the disease we associate with leprosy today.[2] The translation originated from the Septuagint, the Greek version of the Hebrew Bible from the 3rd century BCE, where *tzaraat* was rendered as "lepra," meaning rough or scaly. Subsequent English translations connected *lepra* to leprosy. However, in ancient Greece, what we now call leprosy was known as elephantiasis.[3]

While rabbinic writings from the 1st to 6th century CE extensively discuss *tzaraat*, no actual cases of the disease were recorded during that time. These writings hypothesize about it, similar to the detailed sacrificial laws even after the temple's destruction. Upon closer examination, it becomes apparent that *tzaraat* is not primarily a medical condition but rather a spiritual ailment. Its physical symptoms likely manifest as a reflection of deep-seated spiritual issues.

To comprehend *tzaraat* as a spiritual malady, one needs to recognize the linguistic similarity between a person with *tzaraat* (a *metzorah*) and someone dwelling in a *meitzar*. *Tzaraat* could represent a spiritual affliction stemming from a *Mitzrayim* mindset, even when physically free. In Yiddish, *tzaraat* could be seen as the ailment of *tzuris*, or distress. Expanding on this concept, *tzaraat* might be the affliction of remaining in *Mitzrayim* emotionally, even when physically removed.

The first individual in the Bible afflicted by *tzaraat* is Moses. He initially lacks confidence and faith in God, resembling a slave in Egypt. When God instructs him to redeem the Israelites, Moses skeptically asks, "What if they don't believe me?" (Exod 4:1). God responds by manifesting *tzaraat* on Moses' hand, covered in snowy white scales. After Moses places his hand back into his bosom and takes it out, the affliction disappears, signifying his renewed faith.

Miriam, Moses' sister, also endures a case of *tzaraat* after she disparages Moses' wife for being of Cushite descent. In an ironic twist, she turns snow white as a punishment for ridiculing her sister-in-law's blackness. A typical interpretation equates a *metzorah*

2. Levine, *Leviticus*, 76–77.

3. Biblical Archaeology Society, "Skin Diseases."

(one who suffers from *tzaraat*) with someone who is a *motzei shem ra* (a slanderer who tells rumors about others) (Midrash Tanchuma, Metzorah, 2). In fact, commentaries raise a number of bad behaviors that might cause *tzaraat*, including murder, perjury, forbidden sexual relationships, arrogance, theft, and envy (Arakhin 16a). Put another way, when we act as if we are still living in Egypt, a people without the Torah that was only revealed to them in their freedom, we develop this spiritual malady.

Many Holocaust survivors faced enduring emotional and spiritual imprisonment long after the Holocaust ended. The compounded effects of their trauma, stresses, and a lack of social support heightened the prevalence of post-traumatic stress among them. Research on aging survivors suggests that post-traumatic stress disorder (PTSD) rates could range between 46 percent and 55.5 percent.[4] Primo Levi, an Italian Jew who endured the atrocities of Auschwitz, experienced profound psychological distress following his release. His spiritual turmoil was deepened by his experiences; as he confided to his biographer Ferdinando Camon, "Auschwitz exists, so God cannot exist. I search for a resolution to this dilemma, yet it eludes me."[5] This spiritual crisis mirrored the experiences of the Israelites after their exodus from Egypt. Forty years post-liberation, Levi tragically ended his life, an act widely interpreted as suicide. Elie Wiesel, another survivor and author, poignantly observed, "Primo Levi died at Auschwitz forty years later."[6] Were Levi to have been asked the question "*Ayekah*, where are you?," he would likely have been in Auschwitz (*Mitzrayim*) for the forty years following his liberation, just as the Israelites brought Egypt with them during the forty years of wandering in the *Midbar*. Levi's death was an extension of the suffering he endured, highlighting his identity as a victim of the Nazis who succumbed to suicide rather than merely a suicide victim.

These episodes illustrate that one can physically leave Egypt but still carry emotional and spiritual remnants of *Mitzrayim*,

4. Yehuda et al., "Impact of Trauma," 1815–18.
5. Levi, *Conversations with Primo Levi*, 68.
6. Kirsch, "Primo Levi's Suicide."

manifested sometimes physically through *tzaraat*. Just as stress and anxiety can manifest as physical symptoms like headaches, nausea, or muscle stiffness, *tzaraat* in the Bible appears to behave psychosomatically. Treating the physical symptoms alone is insufficient; addressing the spiritual root causes is essential to alleviate this "Egyptian" malady.

THE *MEITZAR*- CALLING FROM THE PIT

מִן־הַמֵּצַר קָרָאתִי יָּהּ עָנָנִי בַמֶּרְחָב יָהּ׃

From the narrow space I called to *Yah* (God); *Yah* (God) answered me from the wide expanse

—Ps 118:5

Ben, one of my congregants, has felt alone and in a pit since his wife Nancy died from cancer. Ben had always been somewhat of a curmudgeon, but the pain of loss exacerbated this mindset. He frequently uses verses from the Hebrew Bible to remind me of the state of depression that he's in. After I wish him a "Shabbat shalom" (may you have a Shabbat of peace) on a Saturday morning, he responds, "שָׁלוֹם וְאֵין שָׁלוֹם you say peace, there is no peace" (Ezek 13:10). He used to be our regular Torah reader on Saturday morning, but his participation has declined due to his deteriorating physical health. The one part of the service that he sings full-blast occurs once a month when we read a section called "Hallel" (praise). As a part of Hallel, we read Ps 118, which includes Ben's favorite line from the liturgy: "From the *Meitzar* (the narrow place) I call to *Yah* (God), and from the expanse, *Yah* (God) answered me." Ben reminds me constantly that he's in the first part of this line from Psalms but not the second. That is, he dwells in the *Meitzar* and cries to God, but he's still waiting for God to answer back.

Ben is not alone. Throughout the Bible, we find individuals trapped in either a physical or metaphysical pit, seeking to be extricated from their hole. The psalmist calls out to God from a place of despair over and over again, waiting to be heard, pleading for direction and guidance. In my *tzar* (distress) I cried to my God" (Ps 18:7), he writes in a different psalm. Still again, the psalmist writes, "I am considered as one who goes down into the pit, I am but a helpless man" (Ps 88:5). Contrary to how it may feel, the pit is not the place where God has abandoned us; it's the place where God hears us better. Yet God does not answer us always while we're in the pit but rather from the place the Psalms calls the "*merchav,*" the expansive place. The reason why we recite this psalm at a time of Hallel—a liturgy of joy and praise—is because we should see ourselves as having been rescued and now in the *merchav*, able to feel God's presence

The concept of the *meitzar* and the *merchav* might originate biblically, yet they resonate universally. I've counseled countless individuals who feel suffocated by constraints of financial distress, marital acrimony, loneliness, and career troubles. I can't imagine a single person going through life without stumbling at some point and falling into the *meitzar.* The biblical narrative replays this motif regularly because it's ubiquitous to the human experience. Jonah's story, which we will explore next, provides yet another compelling perspective on this theme, shedding light on the transformative power of confronting one's own *meitzar* or pit, and finding a way to climb out to the *merchav*, the expanse where we can hear God's response.

When the prophet Jonah is summoned to deliver a message to the city of Nineveh, he flees from the divine voice and opts to board a ship headed towards Tarshish instead. During the journey, God sends a powerful storm that poses a grave threat to the ship and all the sailors aboard. Jonah, being the root cause of this crisis, is eventually cast into the raging sea and swallowed by a colossal fish. The belly of the fish serves as more than just a fantastical image; it represents a reimagined *meitzar*, a place of confinement and distress. It is within the depths of the fish's belly that Jonah does something for the first time: he begins to pray (Jonah 2:2). Jonah cries out, saying, "I called from my tzar (distress), to You, God" (Jonah 2:3). Jonah's distress is more than just a feeling—it's the metaphorical belly of the fish and the metaphysical *meitzar* that he goes on to describe in detail:

> You threw me into the depths, into the heart of the sea, The waters surrounded me; all Your breakers and waves washed over me. I said to myself, "I was driven away from Your eye's view; would I ever gaze again upon Your holy abode? The waters overtook me up to my source of life, the depths engulfed me. Weeds wrapped around my head." (Jonah 2:4–6)

Jonah's *meitzar* represents both torment and terror, as well as a place where he feels that God is listening to his plea. As Jonah questions whether he will ever see God's "holy abode" again, he begins to realize that the *meitzar* offers him a sanctuary to open up and pour out his heart to God. His initial fear and resistance as a prophet transform into gratitude for his spiritual awakening. Jonah calls out, saying, "You brought my life up from the pit, O God" (Jonah 2:7). The second the fish spews Jonah out into the *merchav*, God repeats his original call to him, answering Jonah's prayer from the depths of the great fish's belly.

David, the biblical king who ruled in the 10th century BCE, endures numerous trials both before and during his reign over the Kingdom of Israel. He ascends to the throne after being divinely appointed to succeed King Saul, who had relentlessly pursued and attempted to kill him. Once king, David faces opposition from external enemies like the Philistines and the Gibeonites, as well as internal threats from his own son Absalom and the insurgent Sheba ben Bichri. Throughout his life, David repeatedly finds himself in dire straits yet manages to overcome each adversity. His experiences and deliverance are poetically recounted in 2 Sam 22, often known as David's Song of Deliverance. The vivid imagery in this song captures David's profound distress:

> For the breakers of Death encompassed me,
> The rivers of ruin overwhelmed me;
> The ropes of Sheol encircled me,
> The snares of Death wrapped around me.
> In my distress (*tzar*) I called on God,

Cried out to my God;
In God's Abode God heard my voice,
My cry entered God's ears . . .
God reached down from on high, God took me,
Drew me out of the mighty waters;
God rescued me from my enemy's might,
From those who hate me and are too mighty for me.
(2 Sam 22:5–7, 17–18)

David's ordeal in the *Meitzar* parallels Jonah's ordeal at sea in its emotional and spiritual depth. Though not at sea, David describes his ordeal as akin to drowning—struggling to stay afloat amid tumultuous waters and fearing unseen predators ready to strike, overwhelmed by the forces arrayed against him. What David discovers is that while it may appear that the *meitzar* is an inescapable abyss, the first step to extricating ourselves is to call out to God from the depths. God may not throw us a rope or pull us up, but when through our own volition we climb out of the *Meitzar,* or from our own metaphysical *Mitzrayim* (Egypt), we might just hear God's response echoing back to us from the expanse of our newfound freedom.

FROM THE MEITZAR TO THE EXPANSE WHERE GOD ANSWERS US

Yonatan Razel, a renowned singer-composer, found inspiration to create the song "Ashira (I Will Sing)" in the midst of a heart-wrenching incident involving his daughter, Rivkah. At the peak of his musical career, while busy working on a new album, tragedy struck when four-year-old Rivkah fell from a second-floor porch during the celebration of Israeli Independence Day. Her critical condition cast the family into the *meitzar*, the depths of despair. The prognosis appeared grim for her survival, even bleaker in terms of avoiding severe brain damage, and most daunting for her chances of regaining mobility. During the ensuing days, Yonatan and his wife, Yael, fervently called out to God for their beloved daughter's healing. Psalm 13, the source of Razel's lyrics for "Ashira," poignantly echoed the emotional turmoil they experienced:

> How long, YHWH; will You ignore me forever?
> How long will You hide Your face from me?
> How long will I have cares on my mind,
> grief in my heart all day. (Ps 13:2–3)

But then, a pivotal moment occurred. Yonatan's brother, Aharon, left him a note that sparked a revelation. It read, "Have you made emotional preparations for the big miracle God is going to perform for you today." And then, the very miracle that they had been praying for occurred—Rivkah began to improve. Her recovery surpassed the expectations of even the most optimistic doctors. While she endured an arduous road, she eventually made a complete recovery. Razel offered that God "showered us with His *chesed* (love), and we know that everything is for the best. Even the most difficult things He does to us are only for our good, but we just don't know how to appreciate them enough." From the *meitzar*, we emerge to the *merchav*, the place of feeling God's presence upon us.[7]

In Ps 13, the psalmist begins in the *meitzar* (narrow place) and ends in the *merchav* (the wide expanse), with a radical transformation of perspective in the middle of the psalm. The psalmist begins with feelings of abandonment, hopelessness, and despair. Without explanation, the psalmist's outlook changes dramatically, culminating in the powerful verse that comprises Yonatan Razel's song:

> וַאֲנִי בְּחַסְדְּךָ בָטַחְתִּי יָגֵל לִבִּי בִּישׁוּעָתֶךָ אָשִׁירָה לַיהוָה כִּי גָמַל עָלָי׃
>
> But I trust in Your love, my heart will exult in Your rescue. I will sing to YHWH, for God has been good to me. (Ps 13:5)

In Yonatan Razel's personal and musical journey, the psalmic progression from the depths of despair to the expansive horizon of trust and gratitude found its profound expression, resonating with anyone who has faced adversity and found solace in their calling to God. When we call out to God from the *meitzar*, God hears us,

7. Davis, "Singing and Cycling for Love."

and the answer often comes in the form of helping us climb out of the pit to the *merchav*. Our role in turn should be to express gratitude not just for being answered but for the blessings the pit teaches us and for the profound blessings of life itself.

YOUR PERSONAL EXODUS

Just as every individual encounters moments of distress and limitations (*Meitzar*), each of us has the capacity to embark on a personal exodus from these constraints. The commandment to leave *Mitzrayim* is both an individual and communal endeavor, but it is not bound by geography. If you have ever had the strength to extricate yourself from an abusive relationship, left a stifling job that ensnared you in daily grinds, or began the road to recovery from addiction, then your experience is a reflection of this commandment. Egypt and its historical oppression may be a distant memory, but *Mitzrayim*, the metaphysical place of constriction and limitation, can manifest in various facets of our lives.

When Joseph, one of my congregants, was first diagnosed with stage 3 rectal cancer, he called me from his newly found *meitzar*—that narrow, constricted place where life suddenly feels smaller. Joseph, a deeply spiritual and optimistic man, had just begun to shift his life into retirement. He had plans to reinvent himself, to move away from the office and into the embrace of his children and new grandchildren. He had started volunteering with local organizations, launched a podcast that quickly took off, and spent more time in his garden. Many people struggle to retire because their identity is too deeply bound to their work—but not Joseph. His retirement opened new pathways for learning, growth, and connection with family and friends.

Less than two years into this new chapter, during a routine colonoscopy, doctors discovered the cancerous growth. Joseph resolved to remain positive, to hold onto his easygoing spirit and his new way of life. After an initial round of chemotherapy, the results were encouraging, and the side effects were minimal. He was in *Mitzrayim*—a place of constriction—but he kept moving forward through the narrowness his illness had imposed. Then came surgery. Though it successfully removed the cancer, the aftermath brought a cascade of complications. An infection, followed by other setbacks, tested his resilience. For a time, Joseph lost his footing and found himself in the deepest recesses of the *meitzar*. From that place, he cried out. He prayed. And slowly, through faith and perseverance, he clawed his way back into the *merchav*—the open expanse—where he once again felt God's presence and could finally utter a *hallelujah* of gratitude. Today, Joseph says, "I'm living life the way I've always wanted to live—as if none of this had ever happened."

Of course, it's easy to sense God answering us when things work out and we recover like Rivka Razel and Joseph. But what happens when we don't heal, when those who we love die, and when we are permanently damaged? Are we still able to express gratitude and feel as though God has brought us out of the *meitzar* into the *merchav*? Do we need to remain permanently in the *meitzar* like Ben? In that these concepts are metaphysical and not physical—that is, they capture our emotional and spiritual state—we posses more control than we often think we have. I learned this lesson most profoundly from a man I met in Israel named Avida. On October 7, 2023, a group of terrorists from Gaza invaded Israel and attacked Israeli villages along the Israel-Gaza border including Kibbutz Be'eiri, where Avida lived with his wife Dana, his son Adar (15), and his daughter Carmel (13). Avida and his family hid in their safe room, designed to shield them from incoming rocket fire but not a terrorist attack of this sort. When terrorists broke into his home, Avida stood in front of the safe-room door to block the terrorists from getting in, but they shot through the door with high-powered automatic weapons, hitting every member of the family. Adar and Dana succumbed to their wounds, while Avida was severely wounded in his leg, which eventually needed to be amputated. Carmel was also struck in the leg several times yet eventually made a full recovery. Avida and Carmel spent close to twelve hours in the safe room struggling to survive blood loss, as well as smoke inhalation, as the terrorists had lit the door on fire. I cannot imagine a more tangible and real *meitzar*. I met Avida when he was still in Sheba Hospital in Ramat Gan a mere thirty-eight days after this traumatic incident, and I expected that he would still be struggling in the pit of *Mitzrayim*. But Avida proceeded to teach and demonstrate that we may be brought into the *meitzar* by circumstance, but our spirit and will alone is what lifts us out. "I am blessed," he said. "My glass isn't half-full, its full. I'm grateful for my thirty-two years with my wife, and my fifteen years with my son." Within him, there wasn't an ounce of hatred, not a whiff of despair, not even a questioning of why, only a perspective that his life is full. I tried to see myself as if I was in Avida's *Mitzrayim*, and the pain was too overwhelming. It normally takes years for people with that kind of trauma to begin their exodus from *Mitzrayim*, yet Avida had done it in less than thirty-eight days. It's entirely normal for trauma to persist for decades before we manage to free ourselves; each person's healing timeline is unique. Yet if ever there was a modern day Moses whose example could guide people to an exodus from the *meitzar*, it is Avida from Be'eiri.

QUESTIONS FOR CONSIDERATION:

1. **Personal Reflection on Liberation:** Have you ever experienced a situation in your life that felt like a metaphysical *Mitzrayim*, a place of constriction and limitation?
2. **Breaking Free:** How did you manage to break free from that constriction, and what did you learn from that experience?
3. **Carrying the Mindset:** Can you identify any aspects of your life where you may still be carrying the mindset of *Mitzrayim*, despite being physically removed from distressing circumstances?
4. **Spiritual Affliction:** Have you ever encountered moments in your life similar to *tzaraat*, where you felt spiritually afflicted or distant from your inner self?
5. **Calling Out to God:** Can you recall moments when you felt like you were calling out to God from a place of distress, from the *meitzar*, and how did you emerge from that situation?

7

Golah

A Rethinking of What It Means to Be Outside the Promised Land

In the early 1990s, a group of Jewish delegates, including several rabbis, embarked on a journey to Dharamsala, India, to meet with the 14th Dalai Lama, the spiritual and political leader of the Tibetan people. The Dalai Lama had escaped from Tibet in 1959 after a failed uprising against Chinese rule. Fearing for his life and the future of his people, he settled in India, which offered him political asylum. Tens of thousands of Tibetans followed seeking refuge, primarily in India, Nepal, and Bhutan.

Decades into exile, with no imminent return to Tibet, the Dalai Lama sought insights from the Jewish people on maintaining their identity through over two thousand years of diaspora, aiming to employ similar strategies to preserve Tibetan culture outside their homeland. Roger Kamenetz, a journalist, accompanied the delegation and documented the exchanges between the Jewish leaders and the Dalai Lama. The Dalai Lama turned to the Jewish people for help. "Tell me your secret," the Dalai Lama requested, "the secret of Jewish spiritual survival in exile." The Jewish community, despite facing persecution, pogroms, expulsions, and genocide, had not only survived but thrived, achieving global leadership in various secular fields like economics, science, and law, while also significantly developing their spirituality and culture during their diaspora.

The delegation shared numerous survival strategies utilized by the Jewish community that could be adapted by the Tibetan Buddhists. Moshe Waldoks pointed to a Jewish inclination towards risk-taking, while Alex Berzin emphasized that "in Judaism there is a great deal of emphasis on the creativity of life and the joy of life. This gives a great inspiration to people to be creative—in education and upbringing, everyone is encouraged to come up with new ideas."[1] "The family is our wheel of life," stressed Blu Greenberg. She continued, "The notion of the family is so deeply ingrained in us, that it is not just the immediate family, our first cousins, the extended family, but the whole family of the Jewish people." Rabbi Ritz Greenberg, Blu's husband, emphasized the importance of incorporating our exile into rituals and prayers: "Every Jew is to be reminded of the exile in the sacred round, during the holidays, and daily life. At the end of every wedding, we break a glass. Why? To remind people they cannot be completely happy. We are still in exile, we have not yet been restored."[2] The eclectic personality of Zalman Schacter-Shalomi suggested the Dalai Lama adopt a Tibetan version of a Seder, a ritualized meal designed to stimulate conversations about identity, freedom, bitterness, and redemption. Each strategy presented was considered for its potential applicability to the Tibetan context, yet the Dalai Lama found certain approaches more valuable than others.

I wasn't yet a rabbi when this exchange occurred in Dharamsala; I wasn't even ten years old. But I often wonder what I might have offered the Dalai Lama. I agree with a great deal of the wisdom shared about how the Tibetan people might survive their exile, but I can't help but think that the rabbis, so focused on exile as a curse, missed the counterintuitive gem of understanding Jewish exile and what it might offer the Dalai Lama. Judaism and the Jewish people didn't survive despite exile; they've thrived because of it. The messages about exile throughout the Bible reflect exile

1. Kamenetz, *Jew in the Lotus*, 222.
2. Kamenetz, *Jew in the Lotus*, 98.

not necessarily as a curse or punishment but the place where we will both discover who we are, and discover the philosophies, cultures, and secular disciplines that would enrich our understandings of ourselves and the world. The exile of the Jewish people was not just a blessing for the Jewish people but for the world.

DISCOVERY

The English term "exile" carries negative connotations, implying a state of forced displacement fraught with adversity and trauma. Conversely, "diaspora" paints a somewhat more positively nuanced image of the Jewish experience outside the land of Israel. The Hebrew similarly carries two distinct terms that describe the Jewish existence outside of Israel, both rooted in the Hebrew letters ג–ל–ה. The first, "*galut*" (גלות), pertains to the forced expulsion of the Jewish people and their state of living in an unwanted exile. The second term, "*golah*" (גולה), delves into the metaphysical, spiritual, or national aspect of diaspora, encapsulating the collective experience of Jews living and thriving outside the Land of Israel. Our focus will center on *golah*, exploring its nuanced significance in shaping the spiritual, metaphysical, and collective identity of the Jewish diaspora.

Looking at the root of both these words of dislocation, we come to see that ג–ל–ה offers a rich secret in its etymology. The root of both means "revelation" or "discovery." When Jewish-American twenty-somethings travel to Israel on the Birthright Israel program, the Hebrew word for their trip has nothing to do with a birthright; it's תגלית *taglit*, from the same root, which means discovery. For Birthright Israel, it's believed that traveling to the Jewish homeland from the American diaspora communities will bring about a discovery of connection to their Jewish identities. In the Bible, it's the reverse. When the Jewish people go through periods of exile, it is their *golah* (diaspora) outside the land of Israel that becomes their *taglit* (discovery). It's in *golah* that the Israelites experience a form of *hitgalut*, revelation. When the Moabite prophet Bilaam journeys to go and curse the Israelite wandering through the wilderness, he has an uncanny encounter along the way. Riding his donkey, a divine messenger obstructs his path, only seen by his donkey, who repeatedly swerves to evade this impediment. Blind to the spiritual figure, Bilaam, frustrated, punishes his donkey for its disobedience by repeatedly striking him. Suddenly, "YHWH reveals (*va'yagel*) to Bilaam that which is before him" (Num 22:31). God doesn't simply open Bilaam's eyes: God offers him the very thing that we find in *golah* (diaspora), that is, a revelation of identity previously unseen. Bilaam realizes that his perception of reality is profoundly limited and his understanding veiled by the physical world's constraints. This divine unveiling not only exposes the divine messenger standing in his path but also imparts an epiphany about the essence of Bilaam's life's purpose. He abandons his mission of placing a curse upon this wandering dislocated people and instead sees the blessing and beauty in the very symbol of their dislocation—their tents (Num 24:5).

Where can our eyes be opened like Bilaam's? A particular piece of rabbinical wisdom that has resonated with me might offer a compelling suggestion. The sage Rabbi Nehorai teaches, "הֱוֵי גוֹלֶה לִמְקוֹם תּוֹרָה, Exile yourself to a place of Torah" (Avot 4:14). When I was considering where to begin my studies as a rabbi, I thought of this verse as a guide. Initially, I interpreted this as an encouragement to physically move to a location renowned for its scholarship and learning—a concept that seemed quite straightforward as I embarked on my first year of rabbinical studies in Jerusalem. However, as years passed and I continued to reflect on this piece of wisdom, my understanding evolved. Rabbi Nehorai (an alias for the renowned Rabbi Meir), relocated from the land of Israel to Babylonia in his later years (Avodah Zarah 18b). Him becoming a *goleh* (diaspora Jew) offers a nuanced interpretation of the above verse. This detail reveals that one of the key pathways to encountering Torah and divine revelation (*hitgalut*) is through the experience of *golah* (diaspora). In other words, "exile yourself, and you will find yourself in a place of Torah." Your location is far less important than your willingness to step into the experience of *golah*.

This theme of transformation through exile is not isolated to the wisdom of Rabbi Nehorai but is deeply embedded in the narratives of the Israelite people. In one of his final messages to the people before his death, Moses foretells a period of exile (*galut*) they will eventually face. He urges them not to lose hope in the face of this destiny. "God is not only issuing a curse but also a blessing," Moses declares (Deut 30:1). It is in exile, he promises, that "YHWH will open your hearts and the hearts of your descendants to love YHWH" (Deut 30:6), and through exile, "YHWH will make you more prosperous than your ancestors" (Deut 30:5). The Israelites had already received the Torah in the middle of the wilderness at Sinai before entering the promised land, and when they are exiled from the promised land in the future, they should come to understand that even in future exiles from the promised land, they are not entering a realm devoid of Torah and revelation (*hitgalut*) but one filled with spiritual revelatory potential.

In *golah*, the Jewish people recognize the imperative to actively maintain their Jewish identity to prevent assimilation into the surrounding cultures. This recognition fosters a deep-seated yearning, a longing that persists as long as any Jew remains in exile and as they await their redemption (*g'ulah*). While some view *galut* (exile) and *golah* (diaspora) synonymously as a punishment for the Jewish people's defiance, this perspective overlooks a crucial aspect of the Jewish experience. It is precisely through *golah* that the Jewish people have consistently flourished globally. Though Israel is their homeland, it is in their diaspora that they truly discover themselves. *Golah* might seem like a temporary state of being that will be negated by a physical return, but such a view falls short of understanding that *golah* is more than just about where you are physically. *Golah* serves as both a physical and metaphysical realm of discovery (*taglit*).

JEREMIAH'S LESSON OF LIVING IN *GOLAH*

In the closing years of the seventh century BCE, amidst the ancient cities of Judah, lived Jeremiah, a prophet whose voice would echo through countless generations of Jewish people. Born in the small town of Anathoth, just a few miles from Jerusalem, Jeremiah is thrust into a world at the crossroads of history, where the fate of nations is being reshaped by the forces of empires around the land of Israel.

As the Assyrian Empire's grip on the region loosen, a power struggle ensues, with new empires rising to fill the void. The Babylonians, under the leadership of Nebuchadnezzar II, emerge as the dominant force, casting a threat of danger over the kingdom of Judah. Jeremiah, witnessing the geopolitical tensions of his time, becomes a lone voice in warning of the impending destruction and exile of his people. Jeremiah laments the social injustices and idolatry that had taken root in Judah, portraying them as betrayals that would lead to the nation's downfall. Yet, his warnings go unheard, his words clashing with the political views and religious complacency of the kings of Judah.

Jeremiah's fears come to fruition as the darkest chapter in Judah's history began—the Babylonian siege of Jerusalem. The city walls crumple and the temple burns, and most of the survivors are forced out of their home to the foreign soil of Babylonia. Yet even in the midst of despair, his message carries a glimmer of hope. *Galut* will not mean the end of the Jewish people. But more importantly, the Jews can shift their perspective from *galut* to *golah* and uncover opportunities for not just spiritual development but the growth of the Jewish people. Instead of wallowing in despair, Jeremiah instructed the people to:

> Build houses and dwell in them, plant gardens and eat their fruit. You should take wives and give birth to sons and daughters; and you should take wives for your sons, and give your daughters to husbands, that they may bear sons and daughters. Multiply there, do not decrease. And seek the prosperity of the city to which I have exiled you and pray to YHWH on its behalf. Because in its prosperity you shall prosper. (Jer 29: 5–7)

Living in g*olah* is no doubt traumatic for many. The desire to return back to the land of Israel overshadows the ability of many

Jews to embrace a future. The writer of Ps 137 expresses a homesickness so strong that it impeded his ability to settle and embrace the blessings of *golah*. Stuck in a bitter mindset of expulsion and exile, he writes:

> By the waters of Babylon, there we sat and we wept as we remembered Zion. There on the willows, we hung our lyres, for there our captors asked us for words of song, our plunderers for rejoicing saying: Sing us a song from Zion! How can we sing songs of YHWH on foreign soil? If I forget you Jerusalem, let my right hand wither. Let my tongue stick to the roof of my mouth if I do not recall you, if I do not elevate Jerusalem to the forefront of my joy. (Ps 137: 1–5)

Embracing Jeremiah's message proved challenging for the community living in exile. Yearning for their homeland and grieving the extensive loss of life during the Judean cities' siege, the notion of welcoming change and finding opportunity in displacement is far from comforting. The exiles perceive themselves more as prisoners than residents of *golah*, a place for potential development and flourishing. The decision to view their situation as *golah* rather than *galut* (forced expulsion) becomes crucial for their survival and adaptation. There's no geographic difference between *galut* and *golah*, but there's certainly a spiritual difference. *Golah* may not be the place that you want to be, but it's often the place that God has destined you to be, and when you've learned to accept that, you can begin to embrace the potential of growth and discovery that you never expected.

EZEKIEL'S VISION OF DRY BONES

The ministry of the prophet Ezekiel intersects with that of Jeremiah, serving the Jewish people during a time of calamity and displacement. While Jeremiah bears witness to the harrowing fall of Jerusalem and its aftermath, opting to stay with a remnant in the land of Israel, Ezekiel's lot is cast with the majority, driven into the heart of Babylonia. Ezekiel's prophetic utterances to the exiles in Babylonia are rich and multifaceted, encompassing the majesty of God, the imperative of repentance, the sanctity of the Jerusalem Temple, the weight of personal responsibility, and the fervent hope for a return to their ancestral homeland.

In a moment of divine encounter, God whisks Ezekiel away from his surroundings to a desolate valley filled with dry bones. This dramatic shift, from the familiar lands of Judea to the estrangement of Babylonia sets the stage for one of Ezekiel's most profound and visionary experiences. This stark vision of devastation has influenced art and music across generations, notably inspiring the iconic song "Dem Dry Bones" by the Delta Rhythm Boys. As Ezekiel surveys the valley, he notes the bones' profound dryness, a poignant symbol of complete ruin and despair.

In a question charged with symbolic meaning, God asks Ezekiel, "Can these bones live?" This question is not just a test but a deep exploration of the potential for rebirth from the ashes of this wasteland. Ezekiel's humble reply, "only You know," signifies his recognition of divine omniscience (Ezek 37:3) but also an inability to see what God wants him to see. That is, the covenant of God with the Jewish people continues even in exile. Just as the bones of the patriarch Jacob were carried up to the promised land from Egypt four hundred years after his death, signifying the enduring nature of the promise made to Abraham, Isaac, and Jacob, so too does the vision of the dry bones represent the unbreakable bond between God and Israel, a bond that not even the harshest exile can sever. What Ezekiel comes to witnesses should assure him that God's covenant with the Jewish people is continuous and unbroken regardless of current circumstances. God then unveils a miraculous scene of reanimation, with each bone connecting to its mate, bound by sinews and wrapped in flesh, signifying the reanimation of the House of Israel from utter hopelessness to unbridled hope.

Ezekiel, witnessing the same spiritual and emotional bleakness that Jeremiah encountered, sought to instill an ethos of resilience. Whereas the people might say "אָבְדָה תִקְוָתֵנוּ our hope is lost" (Ezek 37:11), the guiding mantra—one that the Israeli national anthem echoes—should be "עוֹד לֹא אָבְדָה תִּקְוָתֵנוּ our hope will never be lost." He contrasts the lamentation of lost hope with a defiant declaration that hope is everlasting. Positioning Babylonia not as a grave but as a pathway to redemption, Ezekiel encourages the exiled to look beyond their present suffering and to envision a future rich with possibility, thus spiritually and metaphysically transcending their displacement. Unlike Jeremiah, who advocates for adaptation to life in Babylonia, Ezekiel's prophecies illuminate a path for returnees, teaching that recognizing potential in what appears lifeless fosters a spiritual vitality that transcends the sorrows of exile.

This theme of seeing potential in the seemingly lifeless or hopeless situations is mirrored in a story my mother often shares about me from when I was around five years old—a story I have no memory of yet I don't doubt is true. During the winter, she discovered me in the yard, vigorously stomping on a bush. I was energetically jumping on its branches, intent on its destruction. Upon spotting me, she exclaimed, "What are you doing?" To which I earnestly responded, "Getting rid of these weeds." In my eyes, the bush—a tangled mass of twigs—was unsightly and pointless. Unbeknownst to me, it was actually a rose bush. My judgment at the time seemed justified: the plant appeared dead, devoid of leaves, and, in my mind, required removal. It was January, a time when even the most ornate plants resemble nothing more than withered, forlorn shrubs. When I matured a bit, I acquired something I lacked as a child—vision. Vision extends beyond merely recognizing what lies before us. As Ezekiel enlightens us, vision involves perceiving the unseen, grasping what is not physically present, and foreseeing what time will eventually bring into existence.

Ezekiel's subsequent prophecy using sticks further cements this lesson. Commanded by God, he takes two sticks, inscribing them with the names of Judah and Joseph, and binds them together, a powerful act symbolizing not just the physical reunification of Jerusalem but a spiritual call to envision a future beyond the present. This act, presented to the Jewish people, serves as a tangible representation of the vision of the dry bones, urging a focus on potential and promise over current circumstances. So long as you are able to envision the future, you will be elevated spiritually above any adverse space in which you reside.

STAYING IN *GOLAH* WHEN WE CAN RETURN

Although the Israelites had previously been enslaved in Egypt, the expulsion of Jews to Babylonia begins the Jewish paradigm of *golah*. Even after Jews are allowed to return following the Persian emperor Cyrus the Great's conquest of Babylonia in 539 BCE, many choose to remain, embracing the spiritual and cultural richness that *golah* had brought to their lives.

Those who remain develop some of the most lasting Jewish infrastructure in history. One of the key developments during this period is the shift from temple-centered worship to community-based religious practices. With the temple destroyed and sacrifices no longer possible, the focus moves to prayer, study, and the observance of religious laws as the primary expressions of faith. This period sees the emergence of synagogues as places of worship, study, and community-gathering, which become the new focal points of Jewish life in exile.

The role of religious leaders also evolves during the diaspora. The destruction of the temple and the loss of the priestly class's central role in religious rites gave rise to the importance of scribes and scholars, who would later be known as rabbis. These leaders guide the community in matters of law and spirituality, interpreting the Torah and teaching the people. This leads to a flourishing of religious scholarship and the development of the Babylonian Talmud (compiled circa 500 CE), an opus of Jewish law, commentary, and interpretations.

Despite facing the hardships of displacement and the necessity of adapting to unfamiliar surroundings, the Jewish diaspora preserved a robust sense of identity and unity through their religious rituals, communal organizations, and common customs. It appears that the lessons of *golah* encouraged self-reflection and growth. This capacity for adaptation and endurance was crucial for the survival and prosperity of Judaism during *golah*, establishing the groundwork for its ongoing development and spread in subsequent centuries.

The poetry of the American Jewish poet Charles Reznikoff (1894–1976) engages deeply with the diasporic experience, revealing surprising forms of Jewish creativity within *golah*. Reznikoff, the American-born son of Russian immigrants, writes from New York City while always conscious of being part of a people scattered across the world. His work often turns to Jewish history and Scripture, tracing the emotional and spiritual geography of exile—even in places where Jews once felt rooted.

In one poem, Reznikoff imagines the Jewish people as a vast fruit-bearing tree. When that tree is cut down—the moment of destruction, the loss of the temple—its seeds do not die with it. Instead, they are carried outward by wind and water, traveling across landscapes and seas. The seeds settle, take hold, and sprout in many places at once. Former centers like the land of Israel and Babylonia flourish again; new communities emerge further west along the Mediterranean; even the exiles from Iberia lead to unexpectedly vibrant Jewish expression in places such as Holland and England. The poem suggests that exile did not merely scatter the Jewish people—it generated renewal. What once seemed like devastation becomes the beginning of expansive growth.

Reznikoff's metaphor portrays the Jewish people not as a shattered stump but as seeds capable of taking root anywhere. *Golah* may begin in rupture, but it becomes the ground for reinvention. The poem insists that Jewish creativity often thrives precisely because it has been carried on the winds of history into new soils, where it blooms a hundredfold.[3]

WHAT DEFINES A HOUSE?

The notion of a house often intertwines with the idea of a home, yet the Bible presents a nuanced distinction between the two. In Hebrew, the term for house is "*bayit* בית," with the letter "bet" symbolizing a house in ancient Hebrew pictographs. Interestingly, while the first word of the Hebrew Bible starts with "bet,"

3. Reznikoff, *Poems*, 215.

the inaugural mention of "*bayit*" arises not in the context of Eden but in the narrative of Noah's ark. This choice of setting for the term's debut underlines a profound biblical perspective on what constitutes a house.

Noah's story, marked by divine forewarning of global devastation via flood, positions the ark as humanity's sanctuary. God's directive to Noah, "Make yourself an ark of gofer wood; of reeds make the ark, and cover it from its *bayit* and outside" (Gen 6:3). This verse introduces "*bayit*" in a context devoid of traditional features we might expect a house to have. Unlike houseboats, which boast propulsion and direction, the ark is at the mercy of the waters, emblematic of a journey guided by forces beyond human command. This motif of drift and relocation, unanchored by a fixed abode, recurs throughout biblical narratives, from Abraham's nomadic life across ancient landscapes to Jacob's vagabond existence.

The essence of a home, as these narratives suggest, transcends the physical structure of a dwelling. Instead, it is imbued with the presence of family, friends, and community—the irreplaceable and most valuable aspects of life. My father, grappling with the advanced stages of Parkinson's disease, felt the sharp divide between house and home. When his condition devolved acutely following a sudden and unexpected medical crisis, he spent an extended stay in the hospital, followed by a painstaking period of rehabilitation. Months later, he returned to the familiar walls of the house he had shared with my mother for four decades. However, the man who returned was markedly changed; his ability to walk had been stolen by his condition, necessitating his confinement to the ground floor. The living room, once laid out with couches, chairs, a piano, and even a harpsichord, was stripped of most of its traditional decor and reimagined as a makeshift bedroom and living space, reconfigured to accommodate his new limitations.

Even though he was living in his house, he spent most of his time with a revolving door of caregivers whose names he often struggled to remember. What was once a high-caliber rabbinic mind had gradually diminished, losing its once-remarkable ability to think and reason with cogency and precision. His struggle with delirium and a profound sense of disorientation became daily battles. "Where do you think you are?" I would gently probe when confusion clouded his eyes. He would respond by saying, "I know I'm in what appears to be my house, but I don't understand where I am." His responses, woven with threads of delusion, painted a picture of a man lost within his own house, perceiving it as an alien space. "None of you understand," he would insist. Attempts at grounding him in our shared reality often fell short. His experience of the world differed significantly.

Acknowledging this painful truth, I explained to him that the house that had been his home for the better part of his life was still the same house, but it seemed that he could no longer see it as his home, just a room in the house where he passed the time. His fondness for the house and those within its walls never waned, but his ability to engage with both the space and his loved ones was profoundly diminished. He nodded, his features softening as a visible sigh of relief escaped him. His eyes, previously tense with frustration, now mellowed. His face resonated a complex mix of emotions but foremost an expression of *hineini*. "I think you understand me better than I understand myself," he responded. His delusions were still his reality, and he couldn't flip a switch and understand that they weren't real. After all, they were real—for him. Gradually, he began to understand the invisible forces shaping his disconnect from the sense of home once found within these walls. This was, in essence, what it means to be in exile even as you sit in the very place that you once called home. Home depends not on space but upon the connections we develop in place.

The very way the Israelites are referred to and refer to themselves in the Bible highlights this concept. In Hebrew, the Israelites are often called "*Beit Yisrael*," or the house of Israel, illustrating that home is a state of communal unity rather than the specific geographic locale in which they reside. Yes, the Israelites are often called "*Am Yisrael,*" the people of Israel. Many peoples throughout the Bible are also referred to as "*am*"—which means a people or a nation—or "*goy*," another term used to describe the peoples of the world. But only the Jewish people are ever described as being a "*bayit*," house. "*Beit Yaakov*, house of Jacob, let us go by the light of God" (Isa 2:5). "I brought you close to me the whole of *Beit Yisrael* (House of Israel), the whole of *Beit Yehudah* (House of Judah)" (Jer 13:11). The Jewish people are not just a people: we are a *bayit*, a home when we are with each other, even when we're not in the holy lands central to the Jewish experience. This perspective resonates even in times of exile, as the Israelites in *golah* discover. Jeremiah's counsel to build homes and live fully in a foreign land envisions a universal ability to create a sense of home irrespective of location. A familiar sentiment puts it this way: I'm home as long as I'm with you. For the Jewish people, that becomes "I'm home as long as I'm with Jews." The biblical narrative imagines a house, or "*bayit*," not merely as a physical entity but a space filled with love, community, and the essence of togetherness, making any place a home as long as these elements are present.

GALUT EVEN IN HOMELAND

It might seem contradictory to imagine a Jew experiencing exile even as they are living in the land of Israel. But when we understand the metaphysical nature of *golah*, we can begin to embrace this idea as a sacred paradox. My professor in rabbinical seminary, Rabbi Eugene Borowitz (of blessed memory), once made a statement that I have continuously turned over and over in my head. He wrote, "Anybody who cares seriously about being a Jew is in Exile and would be in Exile even if that person were in Jerusalem."[4] To further his point, he insisted that "indeed, exile might be even worse for a Jew in the state of Israel because one expects more of it and of Jews as masters of their own household than of Jews elsewhere."[5] To Rabbi Borowitz's point, since *golah* began in the 6th Century BCE, it has become a part of Jewish identity and experience wherever a Jew might be.

4. Borowitz, "What We Learned."
5. Borowitz, "What We Learned."

Rabbi Borowitz was an ardent Zionist, believing the land of Israel constitutes the Jewish spiritual, cultural, and political homeland for the Jewish people. Yet unlike many Zionists who founded the State of Israel, Rabbi Borowitz championed the coexistence of the diaspora with the Jewish homeland. An often-used ideological thread within Zionist thinking is "*shlilat haglut*," the negation of exile, a concept generally understood as the need for all Jews worldwide to move to the State of Israel. The radical and political Zionist Ze'ev Jabotinsky famously remarked, "Eliminate the Diaspora, or the Diaspora will surely eliminate you!"[6] But those with a more spiritual and religious bent tend to recognize the fundamental function of *golah,* that is, the importance of *golah* being a key ingredient in the development of Judaism and Jewish identity, as well as a necessary component of bringing about an ultimate messianic redemption (*g'ulah).* In this way, the negation of exile might very well be the negation of Judaism. *Golah* has become intertwined in the fabric of Jewish experience, whether inside or outside the land of Israel.

As an American rabbi living in *golah,* I'm a part of the long line of Jews living outside Israel with no plan of uprooting my life and moving there. Despite this, my spiritual bond with the land and its people remains unshakable. I've played with the tension in my head between relocating my life to Israel and continuing my calling as a rabbi to the American Jewish community. I often find my thoughts deeply intertwined with Israel. But the opportunity to return to Israel doesn't necessitate that we do. Just as many of the Jews exiled to Babylonia after the destruction of Jerusalem chose to establish Babylonia as their permanent home even after presented with the opportunity to return, I believe my role as a rabbi is to serve the Jewish people of the *golah.* I will never abdicate my continued connection to the land of Israel, and will visit frequently and even for extended periods of time, but for the foreseeable

6. This statement, commonly attributed to Ze'ev (Vladimir) Jabotinsky, does not appear in any verified writings or speeches by Jabotinsky. Its precise origin cannot be established, and it is best understood as an apocryphal formulation or later paraphrase of broader Zionist critiques of diasporic life.

future, I have two homes: the first where I live and the other, my ancestral homeland.

Champions of the diaspora like myself understand the negation of the exile through a different lens. We reject the idea of *galut* (exile) as applicable to our Jewish lives, opting instead to see ourselves in *golah.* One should not conflate *golah* (diaspora) with *galut* (exile) and believe that since the State of Israel exists, there is no need for any kind of Jewish existence other than within the Jewish homeland. Doing so not only rejects a successful and thriving diaspora but the very blessings that come along with it.

THE PROMISED LAND AND EDEN ARE NOT THE SAME

The Bible elevates the land of Israel—also known as Canaan, the promised land, the land of milk and honey, Zion, and Judea—to a revered status, leading some to equate this sacred geography with the garden of Eden. This misconception persists despite the understanding that Eden belongs to a metaphysical dimension, fueling the belief that proximity to Israel enhances one's likelihood of experiencing Eden. Despite the profound spiritual connection many hold with Israel, and the myriad of names that celebrate its significance, the reality is that Eden and Israel are distinctly separate entities. Experiencing Eden in Israel does not inherently offer any special advantage in accessing the garden's wonders. One of Eden's most magical aspects is its universality; it can be found anywhere, from the depths of exile to the heart of *Mitzrayim* (Egypt).

Life's journey takes us on a circuitous route from Egypt to the wilderness, towards the promised land, into exile, and back to where we started. Along this path, we find glimpses of Eden wherever we are and everywhere between. We experience moments of spiritual delight that can elevate us even higher than our highest highs and bring us out of the depths—even just momentarily—from the worst physical places in the world. It's entirely possible to live a life devoid of Eden's delight, even within the borders of Israel. When we find ourselves momenting at the gates of the garden, our challenge is not only to recognize where we are but also to internalize the profound significance of the moment we are living in.

THE FUTURE OF TIBETAN EXILE

Envisioning a future where the Dalai Lama and the Tibetan exiles return to their homeland seems an unlikely near future, given the attitude of the Chinese government and the massive migrations following the 1959 uprising. Exile, with its harrowing dislocation, demands a profound reimagining of our ties to the physical realm. Amidst the tumult, the Jewish narrative offers a beacon of resilience, illustrating how to thrive beyond the borders of a homeland. Family, ritual, and faith stand as pillars of Jewish identity, anchoring us regardless of geography. Yet, it is the profound realization that the essence of Israel transcends its soil, residing instead in the spirit of its people, that fuels our perseverance in *golah* (diaspora) or within the homeland itself.

Central to the Jewish experience is the recognition of *golah* as a crucible for *taglit* (discovery) and *hitgalut* (revelation), a sacred realm where we are destined to uncover our true selves and deepen our understanding of our faith and identity. In this longing for return, we trust that this is precisely where God intended us to be: a place where our souls might unfurl, revealing layers of Jewishness and spirituality previously unexplored. *Golah*, then, is not merely about survival; it's a rich soil for growth, a reflection of the idea that home is not confined by walls but exists as a domain of connection, spirit, and community.

The concept of home in this light becomes dynamic, a fluid space that transcends the need for physical structures, guided by the realization that our spiritual and communal bonds provide shelter far more profound than any edifice. This perspective reframes the trauma of expulsion as a call to resilience, a journey from *galut* (exile) to *golah* (diaspora), where the challenges of displacement become opportunities for transformation and enlightenment. In this journey, we find the essence of enduring strength: the ability to see beyond immediate loss to the potential for discovery, connection, and the creation of a home that resides in the heart of a community, wherever it may wander.

QUESTIONS FOR CONSIDERATION:

1. ***Golah*:** How does the concept of "*golah*" challenge or enrich your understanding of facing displacement or change in your own life?
2. **Be a *Goleh*:** In the context of Rabbi Nehorai's advice to "exile yourself to a place of Torah," how do you interpret the role of environment in personal learning?
3. **Living in *Golah*:** Jeremiah encourages the exiles to build and thrive in their new setting. How have you applied this paradigm when you've wound up in a place that wasn't where you desired to be?
4. **Bayit:** The biblical distinction between *bayit* and home suggests a deeper sense of belonging beyond physical spaces. How do you define "home" in your life, and how does this shape your sense of identity and community?

8

Meeting at the Well

In the arid, sunbaked region of Israel, water is more than just a scenic backdrop. Whether you're sitting by the beaches along the coast of the Mediterranean, or gazing out from the rolling hills of the Galilee onto the freshwater reservoir of the Kineret (also known as the Sea of Galilee), you'll find bodies of water strewn through the landscape. Waterscapes throughout the land are diverse, from the Dead Sea, where the hyper-salinity is inhospitable to all aquatic life, to the Red Sea's bustling coral ecosystems teeming with creatures and the refreshing drinking waters of the Jordan River. Water courses through the veins of the land of Israel, especially within the stories of the Bible.

Author Seth Siegel describes the Bible as a "moisture-suffused document," pointing out that the word "dew" is mentioned thirty-five times, the word flood sixty-one times, and the word "water" itself six hundred times.[1] Prayers for rain in the Jewish tradition underscore water's vital importance for survival in this parched region, where rain is a blessing that nurtures the earth and sustains its inhabitants. The rains were the primary life source, especially in a dry land where rain was infrequent—and non-existent during the summer months.

1. Siegel, *Let There Be Water*, 7.

Water touched every facet of life in ancient Israel: it quenched thirst, nourished crops, sustained livestock, and was essential for cooking and cleanliness. People would have collected water from natural sources such as free-running streams, or springs, but in many desert areas, natural bodies of clean water were sparse. A daily blessing reminds us of the unseen aquifers beneath the ground that promise endless springs for those willing to seek them.

בָּרוּךְ אַתָּה ה׳ . . . רוֹקַע הָאָרֶץ עַל הַמָּיִם:

Blessed are You, Who spreads the earth above the waters.

This prayer reminds us that under every part of the land, an endless supply of fresh water sits waiting to quench the thirst of humanity and the land. This life-source is readily available to anyone willing to dig deep.

A distinct and profound variety of water is found within biblical literature, known as "*mayim chayim*," or living waters. These waters are not merely essential for physical survival; they also nourish our souls. While the term typically evokes the image of flowing streams, lakes, or oceans, it extends further to encompass the Torah and teachings that sustain the spirit. This concept underscores the vital connection between spirituality and the nurturing that arises from a vibrant relationship with faith and community. The prophet Isaiah poignantly conveys this idea, inviting the Israelites with the words "let all who are thirsty come and drink" (Isa 55:1). Here, Isaiah speaks of *mayim chayim*—spirituality and the wisdom of the Torah—that sates the soul's thirst in ways mere water cannot. We often regard water as solely a means to satisfy physical thirst, yet it embodies something far richer. In a similar vein, the Hebrew prophet Jeremiah admonishes the Israelites for constructing cisterns to hold water while neglecting the vessels necessary for capturing *mayim chayim.* He declares, "For My people have committed a double wrong: They have abandoned Me, the Fountain of living waters, and carved out for themselves cisterns, broken cisterns that cannot even hold water" (Jer 2:13). This imagery suggests that a deeper truth lies beneath the surface of *mayim chayim*. You may think you're living, but perhaps you're simply alive. What's the difference? The aimless wanderings of life hold little meaning without a sacred purpose—or at least a clear sense of direction. When we tap into the source of *mayim chayim*, we do more than quench our thirst; we connect with a deep wellspring that anchors us in purpose

The biblical narrative casts wells as sites of vibrant community and spiritual centers. Young women typically had the daily chore of drawing water from wells to supply the family household. Wells in rural villages of the biblical landscape were communal structures, centralized in an open location where women would gather and socialize. The same holds true today for women who bear the same well-drawing responsibilities in tribal African villages. The well, and sometimes even the river, become the place of social connection for women. There's an apocryphal story of how tribal women in a remote part of the world would gather by a river each day to wash clothes and linens. Gradually, washing machines were introduced to the village, and before long, most households had access to one. People started to realize that not only were their clothes becoming cleaner, but an unexpected phenomenon was occurring: a widespread increase in depression among the women of the village. The cause was at first a mystery. What had changed? The culprit was the washing machine itself. It had inadvertently disrupted the women's daily ritual of fellowship, the sharing of burdens both physical and emotional.[2] The riverbank had been a central pillar of community and connection that was now lost. The perceived secondary function of the well, or the river, is actually the primary function—bringing people together. Similarly the water itself, might not be about potable water but about "*mayim chayim*," living water.

In contemporary American workplaces, the water cooler has emerged as a central point for social interactions. The act of getting a drink becomes secondary to the opportunity it presents for casual exchanges. This phenomenon is humorously captured by Dwight Schrute, a character from the popular TV comedy series

2. This story is often incorrectly attributed to Brené Brown's book *Braving the Wilderness*, but the origin of the story is unknown.

The Office, who observes that "studies have shown that more information gets passed through water cooler gossip than through official memos." Highlighting the importance of such informal communication channels, Dwight laments his disadvantage due to his habit of bringing his own water to work. In an attempt to overcome this, he unsuccessfully tries to relocate the water cooler next to his desk, only to find that its presence there is too intrusive.[3] We are beings of connection, designed for community, for forging bonds, and for mutual care. What Dwight discovered is what the Bible teaches about the well—the space that brings people together in profound relationship and community is more than just a physical life source, it nourishes the human need for deep connection. The place to go to experience *hineini* is none other than the well. As you draw water from its depths, you may discover that you are not merely retrieving a refreshing drink but also unearthing "*mayim chayim*"—living waters that nourish the soul.

THE WELL OF ABRAHAM

On the periphery of Beersheba, a contemporary city in Israel with ancient roots, lie two wells believed to be at least 3,500 years old, dating back to the era of Abraham. Encircled by a visitor center, these ancient wells invite guests to gaze into their depths, which stretch down to water hidden approximately thirteen meters below the surface in the desert. Edward Robinson, a notable archaeologist, visited the site in 1838 to document the Holy Land. A first-edition copy sits on my bookshelf, and has become a guide for me to unpack early archeology in Israel. Robinson observed in 1838 that:

> Near its northern edge, adjacent to the bank, sit two deep wells known as Bir es-Seba', the ancient Beersheba. The water within is both pure and plentiful . . . Around each well lie stone drinking troughs for camels and flocks, likely similar to those used historically for the livestock

3. *Office*, "Alliance."

> grazing on nearby hills. The curb-stones show deep wear marks from the ropes used to draw water by hand.[4]

These wells are commonly called the Wells of Abraham, not merely for their historical ties to his era but also due to the belief that they are the exact wells Abraham dug, as mentioned in Genesis. According to the Scripture, Abraham settled in the Negev desert and dug a well, which was then seized by the Philistines from Gerar. After a dispute with King Abimelech of Gerar over the well (*be'er*), which the king claims ignorance of his servants' actions, they both swear an oath (*shvuah*) over it, leading to the reconciliation of the well to Abraham. This event leads to the naming of the place as Beersheba, symbolizing a landmark of peace and mutual respect between Abraham and the people of Gerar. The well at Beersheba's edge today is believed to be that very well (Gen 21).

In 1979, Egyptian President Anwar Sadat visited Israel to sign a peace agreement with Israeli Prime Minister Menachem Begin, including a visit to Beersheba. Sadat, who held a deep reverence for biblical texts, suggested to visit Abraham's well. This site, where the common patriarch is said to have established the first peace treaty with another nation, held symbolic significance for the Israeli and Egyptian leaders. By visiting, they aimed to complete a circle of peace, using the well as a historical marker of unity between once-warring nations.[5]

ADDICTED TO WELLS

In the years following Abraham's passing, his son Isaac returns to Gerar, retracing the steps of his father. There, he finds the wells his father had dug—now obstructed by the people of Gerar in a blatant disregard for their ancestors' agreements. Despite this, Isaac prospers in the region, amassing wealth, flocks, herds, and a considerable property, igniting envy among the Philistines. This leads

4. Robinson and Smith, *Biblical Researches*, 1:300–301.
5. Silverman, "Abraham's Well."

the people of Gerar to fill his father's wells with debris, renewing the conflict between Isaac and the city's inhabitants.

Isaac, however, would not be deterred from digging wells. Not only does he unplug the grime that had been used to stop up his father's wells, but he digs new ones too. He names the wells he unplugs by the very same names his father gave them. Isaac's digging of wells further becomes a point of contention with the local residents, and they quarrel over the wells more. Isaac's response is simple: dig more wells. Finally, after digging and digging and digging, there is ample water to spare. We learn that the last of these wells is named Rehovot, which means "wide places," for, as Isaac proclaims, "Now at last YHWH has granted us ample space to increase (*hirchiv*) in the land" (Gen 26:22). This still, however, would not be the final well Isaac would dig. God appears to him after he returns to Beersheba simply to tell him, "Fear not, for I am with you, and I will bless you and increase your offspring for the sake of My servant Abraham" (Gen 26:24). To dedicate this moment of divine encounter, Isaac does what he knows best: he digs another well.

The narrative takes an intriguing turn when Abimelech, mirroring his approach to Abraham, seeks Isaac. This time, however, it was not over contention of a well but simply to recommit to an oath (*shuvah*) between the two parties. Abimelech tells Isaac that "we now see plainly that God has been with you." They make a pact, they eat, drink, and feast, and depart on their ways in peace. Only after peace is established do Isaac's servants finally proclaim "we have found water!"—as if reconciliation itself opened the wellspring of blessing.[6] The water they find isn't about physical water; rather, their wells are only filled with water once there is no longer conflict but instead peace, mutual understanding, and encounter. We are reminded that any physical well can bring water, but when

6. Earlier in the narrative, Isaac's servants "found there a well of living water" (Gen 26:19), though the text records this discovery in the narrator's voice rather than their own. Only in verse 32, following the covenant of peace with Abimelech, do the servants themselves proclaim "we have found water!"—marking a narrative shift from conflict to blessing.

it brings relationship too, it becomes a metaphysical space of meeting the other.

Isaac's well-digging addiction wasn't about bringing forth water from the earth but rather a spiritual search for connection with the people of the land. Isaac may have been searching for *mayim chayim,* living waters, but didn't know what they looked like. It was only after making peace with Abimelech that Isaac finally discovered the spiritual properties of water and his well-digging efforts truly became fruitful.

FINDING LOVE AT THE WELL

How does Isaac learn about the well's spiritual significance? When Isaac's father Abraham seeks a wife for his son, he sends his servant Eliezer back to Haran to find a bride for Isaac from the tribe of his people. After all, Nahor, Abraham's brother, never left Haran, and there his family grew. Eliezer devises a sacred strategy for finding a bride for Isaac. When he enters the city, he heads straight for the well. He prays to God for good fortune and that the first woman who offers him and his camels drink from the well will be the bride God has chosen for Isaac. Just as he finishes his prayer, Rebecca walks by him with filled jugs of water and offers him and his camels drink. Eliezer stands gazing at her, realizing the miraculous interaction he just had. Rebecca's family welcomes Eliezer into their home, and Eliezer tells them all that happened. They agree that Eliezer meeting Rebecca was an occurrence of divine providence. When Rebecca first encounters Isaac, he had just come from the well himself. When they see each other, Rebecca is so overwhelmed by his presence that she falls off her camel (Gen 24:64). Eliezer discovers Rebecca by the well, and Isaac first meets Rebecca when coming from the well. After all, the well is a place of encounter, the place where *hineini* experiences happen. And it should be no surprise then that several biblical figures meet their wives by the well.

Jacob, Isaac's son, travels to Haran in search of a bride and, predictably, makes his way to a well. Upon arrival, he encounters the well, sealed by a large stone, with flocks of sheep nearby awaiting water. It is at this moment that Rachel, his future wife, approaches with her father's sheep. Demonstrating remarkable strength, Jacob single-handedly removes the stone covering the well's mouth and waters Rachel's flock. Intriguingly, the Hebrew word used for "roll" here is *vayagel*, differing from the expected *vayigalgel*. This choice of words suggests a symbolic unveiling consistent with the theme of revelation discussed previously, using the root ג-ל-ה (Gen 28). Thus, Jacob's act of opening the well transcends the physical, symbolizing the establishment of a profound connection with Rachel. The Zohar, a book of Jewish mysticism, imagines that when a person discovers his or her mate at the well, the water level rises (Zohar 1:153a). Put another way, the well is filled when we are fulfilled. Overcome with emotion, Jacob's reaction to seeing Rachel for the first time is to kiss her and weep, illustrating the well as a source of sustenance not just for physical needs but for emotional and relational ones as well.

Moses, too, encounters his future wife at a well. After escaping Egypt due to a death warrant issued by Pharaoh, Moses finds refuge in the land of Midian, where his path leads him straight to a well. It's there that he meets the daughters of Jethro, a Midianite priest who had come to draw water for their father's flock. There, he witnesses a group of Midianite shepherds harassing Jethro's daughter. Demonstrating his inherent leadership and compassion, Moses defends Jethro's daughters, chasing away the hostile shepherds and even watering their flock (Exod 2). Among these daughters, he finds Tzipporah, whom Jethro later offers to Moses in marriage.

The recurrence of the well in such pivotal biblical narratives is symbolic, emphasizing the well not just as a source of physical sustenance but as a magnet for human interaction. Just as we are drawn to wells for water, they draw us into encounters and relationships, underlining our intrinsic need for both water and connection.

FINDING GOD AT THE WELL

In addition to meeting their future spouses at wells, the biblical patriarchs encounter God at these water features too. In an earlier chapter, we recount how Hagar, the maidservant to Sarah (also known as Sarai), flees the torment of her abusive mistress. A messenger of God seeks her out by a well of water on the road to Shur. This divine emissary not only conveys to Hagar that she carries a child, who will be named Ishmael, but also assures her that God witnesses her suffering (Gen 16:11). Hagar invokes the name El-Roi, signifying "God who sees," as she recognizes that God takes notice of her by the well. She aptly names the site Beer-Lahai-Roi, translating to "the well of the Living One who sees me." For Hagar, the well serves not only as the site of the revelation of her unborn son Ishmael but also as the site where she first encounters God. It is not surprising that when she encounters God once more, it is again at a well.

Following Sarah's delivery of her own son, Isaac, she witnesses Hagar's son Ishmael mocking Isaac. Enraged and protective, Sarah demands of her husband Abraham, "Cast out that maidservant and her son, for the son of that maidservant will not share in the inheritance with my son Isaac" (Gen 21:10). Hagar makes her exit, her arms bereft of worldly goods, her entire being steeped in loss. Abandoned and on her own, Hagar wanders aimlessly in the wilderness with Ishmael. In the punishing desert landscape of the Middle East wilderness, she quickly runs out of water. Overwhelmed with despair, she weeps, believing that this situation will spell the end for herself and her son. She places him out of sight and cries, "Let me not look on as the child dies" (Gen 21:16). In the depths of her anguish, as if summoned by her despair, God appears before Hagar, opening her eyes to what was always right before her. What she sees is not a mirage—it's a well. The text reminds us that water lies beneath our very feet; all we need is to recognize that the well can manifest anywhere. By shifting our perspective, we can perceive not just wells scattered everywhere but also opportunities for encountering God in these sanctified places of profound connection.

Recounting Jacob's journey from the Holy Land to Haran, the mystical, and often enigmatic, text of the Zohar offers a captivating reinterpretation of Jacob's iconic dream. In this mysterious vision, the familiar ladder *(sulam)* connecting heaven and earth is replaced by a well (*be'er*) in the midst of a field where Jacob and God sit together. Jacob notices that the water in the well is rising, symbolizing not just spiritual fulfillment but also the ascent of the divine presence (Shechinah) into Jacob's life. Recognizing that the Hebrew words for "water" and "heavens" are *mayim* and *sh'mayim*, that is, the waters that are below and the imagined blue of the sky as waters above, the Zohar conceives the biblical ladder as an inadequate conduit between the two. A well becomes the true bridge between the divine and earthly realms. Just as when we look down at a well, we can't see its bottom but know that our life-source lies at its end, when we look up to the heavens and can't see an end point, we know that the waters that nourish us fall from its peaks. Thus the well becomes a sacred meeting point with God, embodying a divine aspect known as *Shechinah*, which serves as a source of life and spiritual nourishment.[7] Another ancient interpretation of the text reminds us that this well was formed on the eve of the very first Shabbat along with a number of other miraculous things that appear throughout the Hebrew Bible (Avot 5:7). This suggestion implies that the well isn't just a human construct; it's divine in origin.

In the narratives and interpretations that thread through our discussions—from Hagar's profound realization to Jacob's mystical encounter—wells emerge as more than mere physical structures. They symbolize the depths from which spiritual sustenance and divine encounters spring, inviting us to look beneath the surface of our own lives for the presence of the sacred. If we so desire to experience sacred encounters in our lives, we might begin a search for where we might find a well in the modern world.

7. "דָּא כְּגַוְונָא ,וַיַּרְא וְהִנֵּה בְאֵר בַּשָּׂדֶה, רָזָא אִיהוּ, דְּחָמָא הַאי בְּאֵר לְעֵילָּא" He looked, and here: a well in the field. A mystery, for he saw this well above, one corresponding to the other." Zohar 1:152a.

WHERE HAVE THE WELLS GONE?

Since wells are typically a thing of the past, we should ask: Where are the modern-day wells that draw people together? Cities, although densely populated, don't guarantee high rates of meaningful interactions. Social historian Robert Putnam argues that urbanization has fostered a high level of informal social interactions but has made us less prone to communal and civic involvement. Relational living has seen a decline over the years, with people simply preferring to stay home rather than venture out into communal spaces. Whereas the mall may have been a social hub of the past, malls are quickly dying out in American society as people prefer to do their shopping through online sites like Amazon and Walmart. Putnam points out that even at bars—often dubbed "watering holes"—"the frequency with which Americans, both married and single, went out to bars, nightclubs, discos, taverns, and the like declined by about 40–50 percent over the last decade or two. Whether we live alone or not, Americans are staying home in the evening."[8] Within every demographic of American society, social connectedness has declined.

It's not necessarily that modern forms of wells are diminishing; rather more likely is that Americans spend their time in more solitary forms of leisurely activities, including watching TV and social media, neither of which cultivate meaningful interactions. While human beings are social animals and will undoubtedly continue to seek connection and relationship, we have witnessed the overall decline in both the quantity and quality of relationships and the increased investment of time in activities that are solitary. Our time spent in conversation during meals has diminished, our frequency of visiting each others' homes has decreased, our participation in leisure activities that foster casual social interactions has lessened, and we allocate more time to watching screens—sometimes with others—and less to engaging in activities. While the well can take on many different forms in contemporary society, it seems that its allure has weakened. Rabbi Rachel Barenblat's poem entitled "The Well" captures the cultural shift away from journeying to meet others at the well, to remaining at home in solitude:

8. Putnam, *Bowling Alone*, 101.

It's not that the well's run dry.
The walk feels too far. It's uphill
in the snow both ways, and
who has the strength to carry
those dangling buckets balanced
on their shoulders now? I'll stay
on this secondhand chair, wrapped
in my mother's holey shawl.
Make another cup of tea, stay quiet.
Grief sits with me by the fire.
Out the window, tiny birds track
hieroglyphics across the icy ground.[9]

Certainly, solitude and loneliness are not synonymous. For introverts, solitude may serve as a vital source of rejuvenation and energy. However, the enduring wisdom from the creation story of Adam in the Bible reflects a universal truth: "It is not good for a person to be alone" (Gen 2:18). My daughter Lilah often quotes this verse of Scripture to me when I tell her she needs some "alone time." When she gets a little older, we'll parse the distinction between being alone and being lonely. When she eventually goes to college, she'll perhaps read the eminent social psychologist Abraham Maslow, who identified "belonging and love" as essential human needs, emphasizing our intrinsic reliance on interpersonal connections. Even as it's important for us to find time to be alone, nurturing our social connections is becoming more crucial as loneliness rates escalate.

The repercussions of loneliness are profound. Research indicates that individuals grappling with loneliness are at a heightened risk of suicide. Additionally, studies reveal that those enduring chronic loneliness often exhibit physical symptoms, including a compromised immune systems and elevated rates of heart disease. The impact of loneliness on our health might even be as harmful as obesity, as its effects on the physical body are as damaging, according to experts, as chronic alcoholism or the consumption of fifteen cigarettes daily.[10] The worst of the ten plagues with which God af-

9. Barenblat, "Well." Reprinted with permission of the author.

10. Katz, *Heart of Loneliness*, 22–23.

flicts is not, as most would expect, the slaying of the first born. The darkness of the ninth plague, according to many, more severely affects those in Egypt. Not only is the darkness so thick that you can feel it, but the darkness causes "a person not to be able to see his or her sibling," and "people could not even move from their place" (Exod 10:23). Not only are people prevented from gathering together, but they are also deprived of the very sight of one another. This plague is not just about physical blindness; it inflicts a profound sense of isolation and desolation, plunging individuals into the depths of intense loneliness.

The reintroduction of wells into the modern landscape won't cure loneliness, though one synagogue in the suburbs of Chicago, Congregation Bnai Jehoshua Beth Elohim (Deerfield, IL), built a well in the middle of one of their community's social space as the reminder that the synagogue can function as a place of social gathering similar to the way the well gathered people in biblical times. No, it's not very deep, and there isn't water at the bottom. Yet the facade bears a striking to resemblance to Abraham's well in Beersheba, and it serves its function of being a space to gather. The very name for synagogues in Hebrew, *Beit Keneset* (בית כנסת), literally means "the house of gathering." When synagogues were first established during the Babylonian exile, they kept the Jewish community thriving by offering them a social well at which they could continue to gather together. Numerous Jewish organizations have picked up the significance the well played and named their programming or organization "The Well." The Well at Temple Beth Elohim in Wellesley, Massachusetts, has become the name for a social wellness group. The Well is also the name of a Detroit-based Jewish community for young adults and families with young children. At Beth El Synagogue in St. Louis Park, Minnesota, their communal learning program is called "Community Learning at the Well," echoing not just the social connections formed in their classes but painting a metaphor of the well being a place that nourishes and deepens our understanding of Judaism and the world around us. Many Christian communities also pick up on the spiritual significance of the well and brand their churches and programming with wells. In the Gospel of John, Jesus offers a Samaritan woman at a well a type of water that nourishes beyond what the well alone can offer; he uses the familiar term "living water" to describe what the woman can draw from him. Jesus reminds the Samaritan woman that we can be nourished beyond the physical; the well offers us something much deeper than that which quenches our thirst. The well connects us to each other, and it connects us even to God.

Faith-based communities offer more than simply a place to pray; they are one of the richest wells of our time. Synagogues and churches aren't just places where we gather; they're places where we share life experiences together. Robert Putnam suggests that friendships formed within these communities tend to be strong and enduring due to shared values, beliefs, and regular interactions facilitated by religious practices and events. He emphasizes the role of religious institutions in fostering a sense of belonging and interconnectedness among their members, which can contribute to individuals' overall well-being and social integration. In other words, while there has been a decline in religious participation and engagement in faith-based institutions over the years, they still offer us one of the oldest and deepest wells for us to nourish our need to belong and form impactful relationships. There are certainly other places that appear as wells in our lives, each depending on who we are and the culture in which we live, but synagogues and churches mirror another aspect of the biblical well that few other places in contemporary society offer. They are not only meeting places between people; they are also places where we encounter God.

FINDING WELLS IN UNEXPECTED PLACES

By most reasonable expectations, the institution of public libraries should be failing, or at the very least in decline. Since the advent of the internet, more and more people are consuming their information not only from online websites but from electronic books like those found in Amazon's Kindle store. Public libraries have traditionally been known to house hundreds of thousands or even millions of books per library branch. As people began to consume films and music, public libraries attempted to stay relevant by offering patrons the opportunity to check out free copies of CDs and DVDs, but these experiences have also been taken over by online platforms that can be accessed without the need to visit a physical building. While many traditional functions of the public library may be knocking at the door of obsolescence, numerous public libraries are not only surviving—they are thriving. They're not quiet places where librarians demand people speak in soft whispers to avoid causing disruption to the focus of individuals reading and studying; rather they have become modern-day wells, noisy social hubs where people gather and where relationships are forged and cultivated. In his book *Better Together*, Robert Putnam records a reflection of a children's librarian, Anne Ayres:

> "Libraries have changed," she says, and admits that a few people do not like the changes. "You don't get perfect quiet," she explains. "Some older people have trouble with the noise and activity." For most, though, this new style of library is more comfortable and useful than the old one, a place to be known and get to know others, a source of services as well as of books and information. "Now people say, 'I'll meet you at the library,'" Ayres says. "It's a safe place. It reminds me of the old neighborhood grocery store, where the grocer knew everyone and everyone saw their neighbors."[11]

Richard M. Daley, the former mayor of Chicago, referred to the neighborhood public library as the "heartbeat" of the city; he could just have easily called it the city's well. Because just as the primary function of a well might mask its profound spiritual and communal function, so too has the public library's role as a book repository become eclipsed by its function as a community hub.

Especially in large cities, where crowds of people can foster social distance and isolation, public libraries often nurture the intimacy of a small village. Librarians no longer remain behind

11. Putnam and Feldman, *Better Together*, 49.

desks, passively waiting for patrons to check out books; they actively engage with visitors and serve as community catalysts. While some traditional social hubs have waned, public libraries, once perceived as having little social capital, have evolved into modern-day community wells.

MIRIAM'S WELL

Before the Israelites reach the promised land, Moses, Aaron, and Miriam—the trio leading the Israelites through forty years of wilderness—pass away. Miriam is the first to die. Upon their arrival in the Wilderness of Zin at Kadesh, Miriam's death marks a significant turn of events. Immediately following her burial, the Israelites face a dire water shortage.

The Talmudic sages draw a parallel between this lack of water and the absence of Miriam, highlighting her role in providing a miraculous well that sustained the Israelites for forty years in the desert. Miriam, along with her brothers, each bestow a unique gift upon the Israelites: Miriam's well, Aaron's pillar of clouds, and Moses' manna.

The bond between Miriam and water is further elucidated in the Zohar. It narrates how Miriam watches over her infant brother Moses by the Nile, safeguarding him after he was set adrift to escape death. She also led the Israelites in song following the parting of the Sea of Reeds. In recognition of her deep connection with water and her acts of praise, she is endowed with the miraculous ability to provide the Israelites with a well. This well is depicted in a mural at the ancient Dura Europus synagogue in Syria, illustrating streams flowing from Miriam's Well to each of the twelve tribes of Israel. In interpretive descriptions of Miriam's well, it's often described as a rock that issued water (B'Midbar Rabbah 1:1). One commentary notes that you can see this rock if you stand on top of Mt. Carmel and look out at the Mediterranean Sea (Shabbat 35a). Unlike typical wells, Miriam's well is unique in its mobility, moving alongside Miriam for as long as she travels with the Israelites.

Perhaps the notion that the well physically moved with Miriam misses a deeper meaning. It might not have been simply by her merit that God provided the Israelites with the well. Consider the possibility that Miriam herself is the well. Her contribution to the Jewish people transcended physical sustenance: she offered the Israelites *mayim chayim*, the type of water that nourishes us spiritually and emotionally. Thus, experiencing the well isn't just a metaphysical place where we encounter and connect with others, but the very people who nourish us deeply can themselves be the wells in our lives.

Christianity also picked up on the idea of people being the embodiment of the well. The Gospel of John tells the story of a woman finding Jesus sitting by a well. She approaches the well to draw water from it, but before she can, Jesus tells her, "If you knew the gift of God and who it is that asks you for a drink, you would have asked him and he would have given you living water" (John 4:10).[12] Confused by his words, the Samaritan woman inquires, "You have nothing to draw with and the well is deep. Where can you get this living water (John 4:11)?"[13] The woman fails to understand the difference between drinking water from the well and the *mayim chayim*, the living waters that come from individuals who give drink to our souls. Christianity views Jesus as the well in the same way that Miriam serves as a well for the Israelite people.

It's not just ancient biblical figures who serve as communal wells, bringing people together and offering spiritual nourishment that they didn't realize they needed. The best teachers go beyond simply imparting knowledge; they cultivate connections among their students, transforming their classrooms into hubs of community, not just learning. Similarly, rabbis and other clergy don't merely function as preachers or ritual leaders; they foster relationships and fulfill the human need for connection and meaning. Malcolm Gladwell uses the term "connector" to describe individuals with this kind of social acumen. They are people who don't just know a lot of people; they play a crucial role in acting as bridges

12. John 4:10 (NIV).

13. John 4:11 (NIV).

between different peoples and communities, often creating tipping points for social change.[14] Connectors don't need to possess any special holy or divine qualities; they are often everyday individuals who excel at fostering deep relationships. Each of us knows someone who serves as a well in our lives, and each of us has the potential to be a well for others.

WHERE IS YOUR WELL?

Ironically, I have never seen the well that supplies water to my home. While much of the world relies on reservoirs that treat and distribute water through extensive networks, my household draws its supply from a hidden well, its pump buried somewhere in the depths of my backyard. It brings water into the pipes of my house like magic. No one gathers at my well like they did in biblical times; it's simply an expensive water-drawing appliance that has replaced a major function of what the biblical wells offered. In the process of doing so, it has eroded the way the well functioned as a social hub for relationships with others—and even with God.

The spiritual and social essence of what wells represent remains ever relevant. As we navigate the complexities of contemporary society, the challenge lies in identifying and nurturing the "wells" within our midst—spaces and relationships that provide not only sustenance but also deep, meaningful connections. Whether through faith communities, social gatherings, or personal relationships, the search for connection, understanding, and spiritual nourishment is a timeless endeavor.

Miriam's well, as both a literal and spiritual source of life, invites us to reflect on the sources of sustenance and connection in our own lives. It challenges us to seek out and cherish those relationships and spaces that nourish us, body and soul. As we draw from the wells of our lives, we should also consider how we might serve as wellsprings for others, offering companionship, empathy, guidance, and support to those who may be emotionally or

14. Gladwell, *Tipping Point*, 33–55.

spiritually drained. In this way, the legacy of the well—its capacity to bring people together, foster community, and facilitate encounters with the Divine—continues to ripple through time, touching our lives with its life-giving waters.

QUESTIONS FOR CONSIDERATION:

1. **Discovering Your Social Well:** In your life, which spaces or communities serve as the gathering points for spiritual and emotional replenishment?
2. **Encountering the Divine:** Is there a particular place or practice that deepens your sense of connection with the Divine? Describe how this setting facilitates your spiritual encounters.
3. **Quenching Spiritual Thirst:** Can you recall a time when you felt spiritually or emotionally depleted? What or who served as the source of renewal, filling you with hope or comfort?
4. **Romance at the Well:** Reflect on the origin of your relationship with your partner. Was there a "well"—a moment, place, or shared experience—that played a pivotal role in bringing you together?
5. **The Well Within:** Considering the metaphor of Miriam's well, how do you see yourself as a wellspring for others? In what ways do you offer nourishment or support to those around you?

Epilogue
Landedness

FOR MILLENNIA, THE JEWISH people have been seen by many as a wandering nation without a homeland. Expelled repeatedly—not only from their own country in the land of Israel but from numerous countries across Europe and the Middle East, including England, Spain, Portugal, France, Austria, Iraq, Egypt, and Syria—the Jewish people came to understand what it meant to live displaced and untethered from the places they called home. Yet, even during this long history of landlessness, a deep spiritual connection always tied them to their ancestral homeland, the land of Israel. Synagogues were built facing east, oriented toward Jerusalem, where the Holy Temple once stood. Jewish liturgy is replete with references to the return and ingathering of the Jewish people to Israel. The poetry of Yehudah Halevi, the esteemed 12th-century Spanish poet, captures this sentiment perfectly, illustrating the tension between physical displacement and spiritual rootedness in the land of Israel. He wrote, "My heart is in the East, even though I am in the depths of the West."[1]

While metaphysical space and spiritual longing are integral to the Jewish understanding of place, they do not negate the tangible connection between the Jewish people and the physical land of Israel. This bond is not just spiritual; it is deeply physical and enduring. I feel compelled to write this epilogue in response to the

1. Yehudah Halevi, "Libi Ba-Mizrach" ["My Heart Is in the East"], author's translation from the Hebrew.

surge of unfounded claims that deny the Jewish people's legitimate connection to the land of their heritage. These assertions attempt to undermine not just the historical relationship between the Jewish people and Israel but also Jewish identity itself. The exploration of metaphysical geography in Jewish consciousness should never be misinterpreted as diminishing the essential geographic connection to the land of Israel. Since the events of October 7, 2023—the largest massacre of Jews since the Holocaust—anti-Jewish propaganda has intensified, seeking to distort Jewish history and identity.

The physical connection to the land became even more tangible in 1948, when the State of Israel was established, transforming the Jewish ancestral homeland into a haven and refuge for Jews worldwide. After two thousand years without sovereignty over the land they longed for, the Jewish people not only reestablished statehood but witnessed a significant return of Jewish populations from around the world to their place of origin. Antisemitic tropes continue to circulate, seeking to erode this foundational connection, including the false claim that Jews are descendants of the Khazar Empire of the 8th century and have no historical presence in the land. Such claims ignore not only the biblical narrative but also the vast archaeological evidence: Hebrew inscriptions, ancient synagogues, ritual baths, coins, and countless artifacts that affirm Jewish life and worship in the region over millennia.

All of this stands as testament to an unbroken bond between the Jewish people and the land of Israel—a connection that endured through exile, displacement, and longing. It was ultimately reaffirmed with the reestablishment of the state in 1948. Despite ongoing attempts to sever or rewrite this history, the profound evidence of Jewish roots in Israel remains irrefutable and enduring. The ideology that articulates this connection was labeled in the 19th century as "Zionism," a term which was coined by Austrian journalist Nathan Birnbaum in 1890 but describes an ethos embedded within Jewish consciousness since the Jewish people were first exiled from Judea to Babylonia in 586 BCE. "If I forget you Jerusalem, let my right hand wither, let me tongue stick to the roof of my mouth if I don't elevate you to the forefront of my thoughts," cries the author of

Ps 137, a psalm written during this first exile and a long-used poetic rallying cry of Zionism throughout the ages.

We can travel to the metaphysical realm of the Bible wherever it is that we might reside. The Bible's geography is often more of a life-scape of those who read it than a landscape that can be charted on a map. Yet experiencing the land of Israel requires a very real geographic visit, as the perpetual survival and continuity of a nation mandates landedness. Landedness is not merely a practical requirement for survival but a profound affirmation of identity, history, and purpose. The Jewish people's connection to the land of Israel transcends the physical borders and soil—it is a symbiosis of memory, covenant, and future. To walk its ancient paths is to feel the weight of promises kept and yet to be fulfilled. To stand in its cities, forests, and deserts is to know the resilience of a people who have returned, time and again, to rebuild what was destroyed. Landedness, then, is not only about physical presence but about the permanence of hope and the insistence on life, even in the face of attempts to uproot and erase. As the Jewish people continue to face challenges to their existence and connection to this land, the act of affirming landedness becomes a sacred duty—a living testament that exile is not the end of the story, and that the homeland, both physical and spiritual, remains central to the Jewish soul.

Bibliography

Agnon, S. Y. *Present at Sinai: The Giving of the Law.* Translated by Michael Swirsky. Philadelphia: Jewish Publication Society, 1994.

Alter, Robert. *The Five Books of Moses: A Translation with Commentary.* New York: Norton, 2004.

Andersen, Hans Christian. *The Garden of Paradise.* HD Book 12. Head and Heart Digital. Kindle edition.

Ashby, Neil. "Relativity in the Global Positioning System." *Living Reviews in Relativity* 1 (2003) 1–45. https://doi.org/10.12942/lrr-2003-1.

Barenblat, Rachel. "The Well." Velveteen Rabbi (blog), Jan. 10, 2022. https://velveteenrabbi.blogs.com/blog/2022/01/the-well.html.

Biblical Archaeology Society. "How a Generic Term for Skin Diseases in the Hebrew Bible Became 'Leprosy' in English Translation." BAS Library. https://library.biblicalarchaeology.org/sidebar/how-a-generic-term-for-skin-diseases-in-the-hebrew-bible-became-leprosy-in-english-translation/.

Borowitz, Eugene B. "What We Learned from the 1970s, II." *Sh'ma* (Jan 11, 1980) 33–40.

Brach, Tara. *Radical Acceptance: Embracing Your Life with the Heart of a Buddha.* New York: Bantam, 2003.

Buber, Martin. *The Way of Man: According to Hasidic Teaching.* Translated by Bernard H. Mehlman and Gabriel E. Padawer. New York: Function, 2019. Kindle edition.

Carleton, R. Nicholas. "Fear of the Unknown: One Fear to Rule Them All." *Journal of Anxiety Disorders* 41 (2016) 5–21.

Daly, Tom. "Taking the Pain: What Does It Mean to Suffer?" Cycling Weekly, Oct. 23, 2017. https://www.cyclingweekly.com/fitness/training/what-does-it-mean-to-suffer-356111.

Davis, Barry. "Singing and Cycling for Love." *Jerusalem Post*, Nov. 8, 2012. https://www.jpost.com/in-jerusalem/lifestyle/singing-and-cycling-for-love.

Fox, Everett. *The Five Books of Moses: A New Translation with Introductions, Commentary, and Notes*. New York: Schocken, 1995.

Frankl, Viktor E. *Man's Search for Meaning*. Boston: Beacon, 2006.

Gladwell, Malcolm. *The Tipping Point: How Little Things Can Make a Big Difference*. Boston: Little, Brown, 2000.

Goff, Philip. *Galileo's Error: Foundations for a New Science of Consciousness*. New York: Pantheon, 2019.

Goleman, Daniel. *Emotional Intelligence: Why It Can Matter More Than IQ*. New York: Bantam, 1995.

Greenberg, Aharon Yaakov, comp. *Torah Gems: Itturei Torah*. Tel Aviv: Y. Orenstein "Yavneh," 1998.

Hirsh, Norman. "Shabbat Morning 1." In *Mishkan T'filah*, edited by Elyse D. Frishman, 113. New York: CCAR, 2007.

Horner, Matina S. "Sex Differences in Achievement Motivation and Performance in Competitive and Noncompetitive Situations." *Journal of Personality and Social Psychology* 2 (1970) 94–102.

Hughes, Langston. "Harlem." In *Selected Poems of Langston Hughes*, 268. New York: Vintage, 1990.

Docter, Pete, dir. *Inside Out*. Co-directed by Ronnie Del Carmen. Emeryville, CA: Pixar Animation Studios; Burbank, CA: Walt Disney Pictures, 2015. Film.

Kamenetz, Rodger. *The Jew in the Lotus: A Poet's Rediscovery of Jewish Identity in Buddhist India*. New York: HarperCollins, 1994. Kindle edition.

Kato, Teppei. "Ancient Chronography on Abraham's Departure from Haran: Qumran, Josephus, Rabbinic Literature, and Jerome." *Journal for the Study of Judaism* 50 (2019) 178–96.

Katz, Marc. *The Heart of Loneliness: How Jewish Wisdom Can Help You Cope and Find Comfort and Community*. Nashville: Turner, 2020. Kindle edition.

Kirsch, Adam. "Primo Levi's Unlikely Suicide Haunts His Lasting Work." *Tablet*, Sep. 21, 2015. https://www.tabletmag.com/sections/arts-letters/articles/primo-levis-complete-works.

Kushner, Harold S. *When Bad Things Happen to Good People*. New York: Schocken, 1981.

———. *God Was in This Place & I, I Did Not Know*. 25th Anniversary ed. Nashville: Turner, 2017. Kindle edition.

Levine, Baruch A. *Leviticus*. JPS Torah Commentary. Philadelphia: Jewish Publication Society, 1989.

Levi, Primo. *Conversations with Primo Levi*. Interview by Ferdinando Camon. Marlboro, VT: Marlboro, 1989.

Lovecraft, H. P. *Miscellaneous Writings*. Edited by S. T. Joshi. Sauk City, WI: Arkham House, 1995.

Magal, Alicia. "Buber and 'the Mountain Moment': Revelation of a Torah Reader." Paper submitted at the Academy of Jewish Religion, Los Angeles, 2001.

Miller, Rabbi Jason. "Shavuot: The Power of Community." Rabbi Jason (blog), May 28, 2009. https://rabbijason.com/shavuot-the-power-of-community/.

More, Thomas. *Utopia*. Edited and translated by George M. Logan and Robert M. Adams. Cambridge: Cambridge University Press, 1989.

The Office. Season 1, episode 4, "The Alliance." Directed by Bryan Gordon. Written by Michael Schur. Aired Apr. 12, 2005, NBC.

Origen. *On First Principles (De Principiis)*. Book 4, chapter 16.1. In *Ante-Nicene Fathers*, vol. 4, edited by Alexander Roberts and James Donaldson. Grand Rapids: Eerdmans, 1979.

Peck, M. Scott. *Golf and the Spirit: Lessons for the Journey*. New York: Harmony, 1999.

Phillips, John. *Bible Explorer's Guide: How to Understand and Interpret the Bible*. Grand Rapids: Kregel Publications, 2002.

Potok, Chaim. *The Promise*. New York: Knopf, 1969.

Putnam, Robert D. *Bowling Alone: The Collapse and Revival of American Community*. Revised and updated ed. New York: Simon & Schuster, 2020. Kindle edition.

———., and Lewis M. Feldstein. *Better Together: Restoring the American Community*. Kindle edition. New York: Simon & Schuster, 2003.

Reznikoff, Charles. *The Poems of Charles Reznikoff: 1918–1975*. Santa Rosa: Black Sparrow, 2005.

Robinson, Edward, and Eli Smith. *Biblical Researches in Palestine, Mount Sinai and Arabia Petraea: A Journal of Travels in the Year 1838*. Boston: Crocker & Brewster, 1841.

Rowling, J. K. *Harry Potter and the Order of the Phoenix*. New York: Scholastic, 2003.

Salovey, Peter, and John D. Mayer. "Emotional Intelligence." *Imagination, Cognition and Personality* 3 (1990) 185–211.

Schneerson, Menachem Mendel. "Iggeret Kodesh—Mikhtav Be-ḥet Adar Sheni 5717." https://www.chabad.org/therebbe/article_cdo/aid/5019686/jewish/page.htm.

Stern, Chaim. *Gates of Prayer: The New Union Prayer Book for Weekdays, Sabbaths, and Festivals*. New York: Central Conference of American Rabbis, 1975.

Siegel, Seth M. *Let There Be Water: Israel's Solution for a Water-Starved World*. New York: St. Martin's, 2015.

Silverman, Anav. "How the Story of Abraham's Well Continues to Draw Visitors to Beersheba." *Jerusalem Post*, Oct. 25, 2019. https://www.jpost.com/israel-news/searching-for-god-and-water-605556.

Smith, J. Z. *Map Is Not Territory*. Chicago: University of Chicago Press, 1978.

Szenes, Hannah. "A Voice Called, and I Went." In *Eli, May It Never End: Poems and Diary Entries*. Ben-Yehuda Project. https://benyehuda.org/read/2291.

Tanovic, Ema, Dylan G. Gee, and Jutta Joormann. "Intolerance of Uncertainty: Neural and Psychophysiological Correlates of the Perception of Uncertainty as Threatening." *Clinical Psychology Review* 60 (2018) 87–99.

Turner, Victor W. "Liminality and Communitas." In *The Ritual Process: Structure and Anti-Structure*, 95–96. Chicago: Aldine, 1969.

Wahbeh, Helané. *The Science of Channeling: Why You Should Trust Your Intuition and Embrace the Force That Connects Us All.* Newburyport, MA: Sounds True, 2021.

The West Wing. Season 3, episode 13, "Night Five." Directed by Christopher Misiano. Written by Aaron Sorkin. Aired Mar. 6, 2002, NBC.

Wilensky-Lanford, Brook. *Paradise Lust: Searching for the Garden of Eden.* New York: Grove Atlantic, 2011. Kindle edition.

Yehuda, Rachel, Batsheva Kahana, James Schmeidler, Steven M. Southwick, Stephen Wilson, and Edwin L. Giller Jr. "Impact of Cumulative Lifetime Trauma and Recent Stress on Current Posttraumatic Stress Disorder Symptoms in Holocaust Survivors." *American Journal of Psychiatry* 152 (1995) 1815–18.

Zornberg, Avivah Gottlieb. *The Murmuring Deep: Reflections on the Biblical Unconscious.* New York: Schocken, 2009. Kindle edition.

Subject Index

Ancient Document Index

www.ingramcontent.com/pod-product-compliance
Lightning Source LLC
LaVergne TN
LVHW020626100826
845148LV00012B/2066